DARK PSYCHOLOGY AND MANIPULATION PROTECTION 2 IN 1

DISCOVER HOW TO ANALYZE BODY LANGUAGE & INCREASE EMOTIONAL INTELLIGENCE TO PROTECT AGAINST DARK PERSUASION, NLP, NARCISSISTS & MIND CONTROL TECHNIQUES

WESTLEY ARMSTRONG

DEVON HOUSE
PRESS

CONTENTS

Introduction   v

Part I
PREPARE YOURSELF
1. It Starts Within   3
2. Delve Deeper into Your Emotions   12

Part II
WHAT YOU'RE UP AGAINST
3. The People Who Wish to Harm You   27
4. Why Dark Psychology?   32
5. The Dark Triad   46
6. Harmless Persuasion versus Dark Persuasion   56
7. What You Need to Know on Manipulation   70
8. Facing the Facts of Hypnosis, Brainwashing, and   84
   Mind Control
9. Two Sides of NLP   100

Part III
PROTECTING YOURSELF
10. Are You a Victim?   115
11. See It for What It Really Is   132
12. Raising Your Walls   144
13. In a Relationship with Difficult People   159
14. Against Online Attacks   172
15. Improving Your Emotional Intelligence   184

Conclusion   197
Resources   201

INTRODUCTION

We are living in a world that is intrinsically dark and scary. What you see is a fraction of what happens in the dark, far hidden from the naked eyes or, at times, beyond human comprehension. Reports have it that some marketers, businesspersons, religious leaders, cultists, even our so-called friends and relatives can engage in dark psychology to manipulate, mind control, coerce, persuade, and influence us in a way that makes it very easy for them to take advantage of us and get whatever they want from us.

This problem has relatively got out of hand as there are so many books and different forms of instructional media out there teaching people how to use dark psychology to manipulate the others for their own selfish gains. However, the good news is that an equally large number of people, who have now woken up to the realization of these evil practices, are seeking for ways to protect themselves against manipulation, persuasion, and dark psychology.

This book, a practical guide, is specifically written to offer the much-needed help so that people can avoid becoming victims of dark psychology, manipulation, hypnosis, unfavorable coercion, and deceitful persuasion.

In September 2015, a tragedy struck at my former workplace, one of my colleagues—my best friend ever—had committed suicide inside one of the workshops adjacent to the main administrative building. Big Alistair, as we used to call him, did leave a suicide note. "I have let everyone down," he regrettably stated. More enquiries into the cause of this gruesome incident revealed that he had met a dashing, young lady on one of the online dating sites. The strange lady, we learnt, had taken control of Big Alistair's life, coercing him to act on all occasions against his wish.

The comprehensive investigations by the police revealed that my former colleague, following the strict orders of his newfound lover, had emptied all his savings, estimated to be about £45,000, and handed everything to her. However, her demand for money didn't abate until she had forced him to borrow from friends and family members. When Big Alistair couldn't find someone to lend him money due to his inability to repay those he was owing, he turned to stealing from our company's coffers—he was one of the accounting officers. He embezzled a total of £200,000 from our company, giving it all to his eccentric girlfriend!

It reached a point that he had no money on him, no one to lend him any, and he knew that the time to do the annual auditing of our company's financial accounting was fast approaching. He realized he had had no apparent option than to kill himself. So sad he ended his life that way, without even letting his family or friends know! Finally, the news broke out that the weird lady had been manipulating him, using all kinds of dark psychological powers to hypnotize, control, and order him around like a baby.

It is the story of Big Alistair that led to the development of this book. We cannot afford to wait for the next victim to come up before we do something about it. It is quite unfortunate and bewildering that an increasing number of people are still learning hypnotism, dark psychology, and neurolinguistic programming (NLP) for the singular purpose of harming other people. A search on the internet will turn up hundreds of schools and institutes offering NLP courses for whoever wants to learn it. This reveals that the enormity of this problem is bigger than what we had previously envisaged.

What will you do in the face of all these mounting life challenges and risks? Will you just sit down and fold your arms, doing nothing? Well, many people are truly clueless about how to address this very serious issue. This is why this book is designed to help people in that situation. It will not only make you to be fully aware of the things happening around you, but it will also empower you with the right amount of practicable knowledge that you can utilize to protect yourself from evil-minded people.

After the eye-opening circumstance of Big Alistair, I was able to timely intervene and prevent one of my own cousins from going down the same drain. He had madly fallen in love with a lady he also met online and the lady, using some dark psychological powers on him, had requested for his ATM card and its PIN number. I sat him down on the Christmas Eve of 2018, just one day before he could hand over everything to her so that she could go on a shopping spree on Christmas Day!

In another but closely related situation, a successful steel company owner discovered that one of his customers often asked him for goods on credit, even though he was still owing him a lot of money, around £100,000. But the most surprising aspect of this story was that the businessman never had the courage or energy in him to say "No" to his Oliver Twist customer. After asking the steel company owner some thought-provoking questions, I discovered that his so-called customer had been using some dark powers to persuade him. Such an evil customer will keep requesting for more steel products until the amount runs up to, say £1 million and then he would suddenly disappear. After holding series of consultations with the businessman, we were able to confront the customer who later confessed to his evil deeds. He was handed over to the police for proper prosecution.

You will discover, in this book, all the necessary things you need to do to better protect yourself. It is counterproductive to wait until you find yourself in a difficult situation or falling victim to some evil people's machinations or devious actions before you keep yourself and your loved ones safe.

When you are dealing with a manipulative person, the extent of what you could lose is infinite. People have lost valuable possessions, including their own precious lives when they did not quickly realize how dangerous the person they were dealing with was. However, identifying a manipulative person and escaping from his/her firm grip are two different things. Armed with the knowledge in this book, you will be able to quickly detect the traits of a manipulative person as well as doing everything in your power to set yourself free from his/her self-centered persuasion, coercion, and destructive manipulation.

Congratulations that you are one of the lucky people to be reading this! It is now in your power to help someone else by sharing some of the topics that you will learn from this book. Help your friends, relatives, colleagues, and even your neighbors stay abreast of the latest information about the danger of NLP, dark psychology, hypnotism, coercion, and damaging persuasion. You will be happy you did if you could help save just one person's life.

I

PREPARE YOURSELF

1

IT STARTS WITHIN

O vercoming the tricks and traps of hypnotists, heartless manipulators, and wicked practitioners of dark psychology requires some strategic preparations. And it all starts from within.

ARE YOU READY?

Freeing yourself from a cruel person or a group of mischievous people who want to take control of your life for their own personal gains or gratifications is comparable to fighting a war. Unlike the physical one, this battle requires you to be mentally strong and determined. And are you ready?

Asking this question is very important because you won't achieve any tangible victory against those callous manipulators and hypnotists if you are shoddily prepared for it. Do you know what being ready means?

It entails that you are no longer going to be:

- Destroyed by self-pity or getting depressed instead of taking your fate into your own hands
- Blaming others for your problems, but you have already made up your mind to fight it to the end
- Fearful and indecisive about it
- Postponing when to act, for there is apparently no room for being lazy about dealing with an enemy that is coming after everything you have, including your dear life, if you don't act NOW!

MENTAL HEALTH IS INVOLVED

This war requires that you exercise your mental muscles, not your physical muscles. You must exhibit sound mental health to ward off the subtle advances of manipulators and practitioners of dark psychology. What does it mean to have sound mental health? Very simple. You must demonstrate a high degree of emotional, cognitive, and behavioural well-being. You must absolutely be in charge of your emotional and behavioural reflections so that you are capable of handling all stressful and disturbing circumstances that come your way without demonstrating any signs of mental disorders or breakdown.

The adage goes like this: "A disturbed soul is a conquered soul". If you want to be able to stand your ground and frustrate every trick of the manipulators, you must make sure you are not the type who breaks down easily under any pressure. There will be some socio-cultural and psychological pressures, partly instigated by the actions of the cruel manipulators or practitioners of dark psychology whose primary goal is to first destabilize your life before pouncing on you.

Some Early Signs You Should Watch Out For

If you are showing any or all of the early signs of mental health problems described below, you should immediately work on developing your mental health or seek professional help:

- Irregular eating habits
- Suffering from insomnia or sleeping too much
- Extreme social withdrawal
- Lacking adequate energy to carry out the normal functions at work or home
- Occasionally feeling numb or too tired
- Suffering from migraines or other pains
- Periodically experiencing a state of helplessness or hopelessness
- Intentionally abusing substances such as drugs and alcohol in a large amount
- Displaying emotional imbalance characterized by intense anger, confusion, forgetfulness, or irrationally feeling scared
- Showing uncontrollable domestic violence to friends and family members
- Demonstrating extreme mood swings and inability to maintain good relationships
- Entertaining self-demeaning thoughts from time to time
- Stubbornly doubtful of the realities

- Hearing voices and experiencing blurred visions
- Troubled with the thoughts of committing suicide or harming yourself or someone else

Paying attention to the signs mentioned above may help you detect any mental issues in time and find ways to quickly ameliorate it before the enemies strike. If you see another person displaying any of the characteristics of mental-health problems highlighted above, you could be the savior of such a person by directing him/her to seek timely intervention before the problems get out of hand.

You will soon discover later in this book how difficult it is dealing with hypnotists or manipulators when you are mentally unstable, who usually exert social, psychological, and economical pressures on their victims. The truth must be told: A broken person is as powerless as a deflated ball because the air it uses for power has already been sucked out of it. You do not want to be in a powerless situation or see any of your loved ones in that pitiable state. This is why it is imperative that you develop your mental health.

DEVELOPING YOUR MENTAL STRENGTH

There isn't any other way around it, you must take decisive steps to develop your mental strength, making it difficult for those who want to manipulate or extort you through hypnotism to do so. The very first thing you need to do is, with the help of your physician or licensed mental health professional, is to identify the probable cause of your mental health problem(s).

Three Possible Causes of Mental Health Problems

- **Biological factors**: Some people exhibit mental health illness due to their genetic compositions or certain chemical reactions in their brains. This may be caused by some diseases or disorders such as type 1 diabetes, chromosomal abnormalities, Autism, and others. These biological risk factors can also be triggered by several environmental conditions. The brain usually functions improperly when there are certain levels of chemical imbalance in them, or there is dysfunction in the neural pathways responsible for dispersing these chemicals in the brain, such as in the case of anorexia nervosa.

- **Difficult life experiences**: People who go through some difficult life experiences do display some kinds of mental health illnesses. Trauma or past abuse can impair someone's mental sharpness and cause him/her to behave erratically. Take for instance, those who have been homeless for a long time may express some certain asocial attitudes normally seen in a mentally unstable person.

- **Hereditary**: People who come from a family lineage where signs of mental instability are common may exhibit certain levels of mental health problems. When looking at hereditary causes, it is important to trace back the family tree to as many generations as possible.

7 PRACTICAL WAYS TO DEVELOP YOUR MENTAL HEALTH STRENGTH

If you are in doubt about how to proactively develop your mental strength, which you seriously need to prevent instances of being manipulated, hypnotized, coerced, or abused, the following 7 tested approaches for strengthening your mental alacrity will be of special interest to you:

1. **Declutter your mind:** When confused, disturbed, and perturbed, human mind is comparable to a messy gutter through which run some dirty water, rubbish, and particles. You need to systematically declutter your mind. Take every precaution to identify those negative, self-limiting thoughts in your head and gradually remove them from your mind. You can never feel great and enjoy great mental health if you often doubt yourself or put yourself in a position of constant fear.

2. **Be positive:** You need to empower yourself with great positivism. This entails that you should live a positive life, only embrace positive things about yourself and others, and put out positive energy, because whatever goes around comes around.

3. **Coping strategy:** Do not aspire to be the person that runs away from challenges. You should rather be a person that withstands pressures of all kinds but always emerging victorious, successful, and confident. You need to develop some inner coping strategies you will need to handle external

challenges. This is because tough situations won't last, but tough people do.

4. **Be productive:** There are so many blessings associated with being super productive. In addition to helping you focus on the right thing at the right time, it also takes your mind away from useless, negative thoughts. Working hard will help you realize your full potential and become a source of motivation if you succeed at whatever you are doing.

5. **Life-enriching relationships:** It is counter-productive for anyone suffering from any kind of mental health problems to put himself/herself in relationships that will drain their energy and turn them into powerless individuals. Take it upon yourself to start or be in relationships that will build you up. Energy-sapping relationships if they don't kill you, will render you powerless for a very long time. Do something good for your communities and positively connect with others. One good way to remain mentally alert is to help others; You can help those who you perceive are in danger of being manipulated or psychologically attacked by practitioners of dark psychology. By doing this great human service, you are also automatically strengthening your own mental health.

6. **Taking care of your body:** You should get enough sleep and take good care of your body hygiene. Health is wealth, because if your body suffers some illnesses for a long time, it could consequently affect your mental health. Kick bad habits such as excessive drinking, smoking, and nightlife

7. **Get professional help:** When you have done all you can

to strengthen your mental health, but you are still feeling drowsy or down, you can seek help from qualified health professionals. Do not be shy about it; it is better you are outright about it and empower yourself by doing so. Psychotherapy and medications are some of the medical approaches for treating mental health illnesses. Your physician or an experienced mental health professional can gradually guide you through a process of recovery and rediscovering yourself. It may or may not be long, but it is surely worth doing. You will thank yourself later.

PROTECTING YOURSELF

You have accomplished something tangible if you have taken all appropriate measures to develop your mental strength. However, maintaining one's mental health is not just a sprint; it is a marathon. It is something you have to do from time to time.

Surprisingly enough, it is not something you can do on your own. You need a kind of support system to keep your mental sharpness intact. Some people are so lucky surrounding themselves with good friends, relatives, and colleagues who are able to motivate, encourage, and assist them in their daily mental health development. Unfortunately, not everyone is that lucky; some are surrounded by vampires sucking their energy from time to time.

If you belong to the latter group, you will find this book very helpful, like a companion, to constantly guide you in the process to keep your mental health in good shape. You will unearth a lot of information designed to give you that emotional backing that you long desire. More so, you will identify ways to spot manipulators so you can escape from their traps.

It is very important that you constantly learn how to protect yourself from various unseen psychological attacks. It is like learning physical self-defense tactics you can use to knock your enemies down. In this scenario, you are just focusing on the strategies that will equip you with all the necessary information you need to protect your mind from external manipulators, many of whom are close friends, associates, relatives, or even your neighbors.

DELVE DEEPER INTO YOUR EMOTIONS

This is the most important secret you need to be aware of: Cruel manipulators, hypnotists, and practitioners of Dark Psychology often target their would-be victims' emotions. They tamper with people's emotions for the purposes of altering, controlling, and subduing their thinking, realities and, of course, their actions.

Your sole chance of outmaneuvering manipulators begins right in your mind, realizing how powerful your emotion is. If you can prevent any wicked hypnotist from taking over your emotions, you are already victorious.

UNDERSTANDING THE HUMAN EMOTION

So, what are emotions? Many scientists and psychologists have struggled with perfectly defining what an emotion is. Some believe it is just a human feeling, a kind of reflexive response to a specific condition or experience. Others have proposed that emotion embodies both the feeling and bodily reaction to both external and internal stimuli. Whichever definition of emotion you embrace, the fact remains the same that emotion plays a significant role in your ability to live a healthy life, enjoy robust relationships, be in control of your senses, and maintain your personal dignity.

There are six fundamental structures or kinds of emotions: **Anger, fear, disgust, surprise, sadness,** and **joy**. Each kind of these emotions can make or mar you, depending on how capable you are at controlling it. What a manipulator does is tap into your apparent weakness in handling your emotions and deftly use them against you, to decimate your psyche and literally take over your senses or subconscious.

This anecdote will better show you how crafty hypnotists or manipulators work: Mr. A is always full of anger. He often shows anger in his words and reactions to external stimuli. When he comes into contact with a manipulator, all the manipulator needs to do is to amplify his anger in a way that Mr. A will lose his senses, making himself vulnerable to a deceitful manipulator who does not mean well for him but just to use him for his/her selfish purposes.

To further illustrate how humans experience emotions, scientists came up with two mutually exclusive properties of human emotions. They call it **valence** versus **arousal**. In other words, they describe valence as the degree to which an individual feels good or bad, while arousal expresses the degree to which a person feels excited or calm. When you feel extremely good about yourself or your achievements, your emotion is at **high valence**. However, when you are sad and dejected, your emotion is at **low valence**. In the same way, your emotion is considered to be at **high arousal** when you are extremely excited, but it turns to **low arousal** when you are calm and confused.

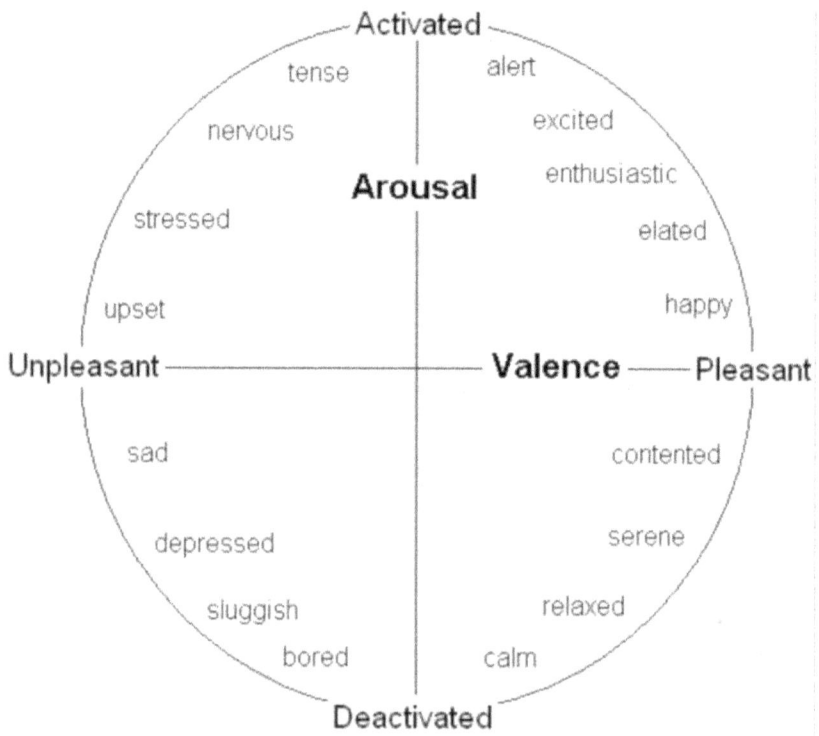

Valence and Arousal: Properties of Human Emotions, diagram obtained from ResearchGate

As indicated in the diagram above, a person tends to become obviously **deactivated** when he/she reaches the state of high valence of emotion. As demonstrated in the anecdote, Mr. A will virtually become deactivated and lose his total composure or consciousness when his anger reaches the highest level. At that stage, it does not take a manipulator any extra effort to dangerously influence or run his life.

Here is the greatest warning: The same evil manipulation can be achieved with high arousal, positive emotion. Take for instance, a man who often loses himself when he is in a company of an incredibly beautiful lady can easily fall victim to any pretty female hypnotist.

You can now see how dangerous the situation is, that both your negative and positive emotions can be used to coerce, control, manipulate, or hypnotize you!

WHAT CAUSES EMOTION?

Normally, emotions are our ways of responding to an experience or event that happens to us or around us. Almost all scientists and psychologists who have studied about human emotions agree that showing emotions, whether sadness or joy, is normal and expected. In fact, they outlined three main categories of emotional triggers in human beings.

1. Common causes: People commonly express their emotions because:

- **They are humans**—every human has a heart that can feel the good and bad, hence they respond exactly to what they feel.
- **Genetics**—some people are more emotional than others.

This is due to their inherited genes. Although environmental and social factors may also play some significant roles.

- **Insomnia**—sleeplessness or lack of adequate sleep can make someone depressed and affected by anxiety. These conditions weaken the immune system and can make an individual so emotional.

- **Tardiness**—not doing enough exercise can make your mood swings dangerous. Good exercise is believed to be helpful in stabilizing one's moods and emotions.

- **Unhealthy diet**—Scientists believe that consuming an unhealthy and unbalanced diet can weaken someone's immune system and make them susceptible to emotional outburst from time to time.

- **Being too sensitive**—Part of humanity is to show love and concern to the others around us. If you are too sensitive, you may find yourself expressing your emotions a lot within a short period of time.

2. Health and emotions: It is not surprising that the state of your health may be one of the reasons you are quite emotional. The following health factors are fundamentally responsible for expressing emotions in humans:

- **Hormones**—Hormones are wired in a way that they can cause both physical and psychological changes in your body and emotions when they are imbalanced. Some of the health issues that may alter the balance of hormones in your body include stress, thyroid problem, PCOS, menopause, birth control, PMDD, and PMS.

- **Depression**—is a typical mood disorder that affects millions of people across the globe. Those who are deeply depressed exhibit high levels of negative emotions. On most occasions, they may feel hopeless, sad, empty, and angry.

- **Anxiety**—like depression, anxiety brings a great deal of fearfulness and anxious feeling into the lives of people suffering from chronic anxiety. They may be tense on most days and have their emotions heightened. They are usually angry and show deep apprehension frequently.

- **Personality disorders**—those who are experiencing personality disorders often find themselves in a situation where it is difficult for them to control their emotions. They are quite sensitive, their moods swing every time they are criticized.

- **ADHD**—Those who are affected by ADHD are known for their hypersensitive and emotional behaviors. They apparently find it difficult to control their focus, feelings, and attitudes.

3. Situational Causes: Certain situations in your life can cause you to experience emotional fluctuations. Sometimes it may be beyond your power to immediately rectify the situations. For example, your emotion may be caused by:

- **Uncontrollable stress**—Stressed people often demonstrate quick mood swings. They are so physically and mentally tired that they sometimes, unintentionally, show their emotional side.

- **Grieving people**—when grieving about a loss, people do not necessarily make any attempt to control their emotions. They will just let their emotions take the best of them.
- **Eventful events in life**—If you are getting married, giving birth to a baby or getting a divorce, your emotions may run high. Several big changes in people's lives largely affect the way they feel and how they reflect on their experiences.

To a certain degree, culture, which is a set of beliefs, norms, values, and attitudes seems to have an overarching influence on how people perceive, receive, process, and display emotions. Why some individuals in certain cultures may shed tears when an elderly person passes away, that may not be the case in another culture. So, all the emotional triggers described above may not be usually applicable to people from different cultures.

DIFFERENT LEVELS OF EMOTION

Individually, we operate at different levels of emotion. What does this mean? Haven't you seen twins that were born on the same day by the same mother displaying different types of emotions when witnessing the same events? This explains the undeniable fact that humans display different levels of emotion, even though they are going through the same experiences.

There are three unique levels of emotions, and they are described as follows:

- **Not showing adequate concern for others:** There are some people who don't necessarily feel concerned about what others are going through, whether good or bad. Even the Bible says that we should rejoice with those who are celebrating and mourn with those in troubles. Have you ever witnessed a ghastly accident where precious human lives were lost, and people were crying? There would be someone there who didn't feel moved by the outpouring emotions around him/her. Such a person had not affinity or chemistry of emotion with the victim. This is exactly how manipulators and mind-benders do; they derive maximum joy in seeing their victims suffer or be in pain because they simply cannot relate to the hardship, they had intentionally thrown them into. Expecting a manipulator to be considerate is like expecting the Devil to become a Saint overnight. It will never happen! Knowing about how callous and evil they are is your only weapon to protect yourself from their tricks and manifold wickedness.

- **Demonstrating extremely high concern for others:** This is the second level of human emotion. I think you can find this outpouring of positive emotions of joy, love, appreciation, encouragement, and the rest from your immediate families and loyal friends. However, you still have to tread cautiously when dealing with people; those who are your loyal friends today might turn into your sworn enemies tomorrow. The bottom line is that you don't want to put yourself in a position that any Dick and Harry can take advantage of you, using you the way they like.

- **Lacking good emotional coping skill:** A person who is too gentle and feeble is considered to be lacking the good skill for dealing with his/her own emotions and those of the people around him/her. You don't want to show the whole world around you that you are weak, feeble, and incapable of managing your own emotions. Manipulators, like a roaring lion, scout around for their next victims, and it would be a grave mistake on your part not to present yourself as a person with a strong personality.

How do I successfully manage my emotions then, you may ask? The first thing you need to be aware of is that your emotions are not only about your physical response to events or happenings around you, but they are also the outcomes of the chemical reactions going in your brain. Millions of chemical reactions occur in your brain, and they could affect your overall emotions. These chemical reactions occur as a result of synapses in your central nervous system. To be precise, emotions emanate from the arousal of the central nervous system. When something happens, neurons in your central nervous system transmit the message via neurotransmitters in your body. Then this will bring about a certain feeling that you will then display as your emotion.

How much control do you have on these chemical reactions that dictate which emotions you will display physically? That's an important question! There are some chemicals in your body that are responsible for these chemical reactions. The main chemicals are dopamine and serotonin.

Dopamine ($C_8H_{11}NO_2$) functions primarily as a neurotransmitter, and it has a huge impact on mood and emotions. If you have plenty of dopamine in your body it can lead to unexpected behavioural problems characterized by mood swings. Dopamine is not man-made; it occurs naturally in your body.

Like dopamine, serotonin ($C_{10}H_{12}N_2O$) is also a neurotransmitter, it mainly works by regulating thinking, mood, emotions, and impulse control. If you have adequate serotonin in your body, it can make you feel optimistic and happy. But if you lack enough serotonin in your body, you can be exhibiting signs of depression, anger, and anxiety.

While dopamine cannot be produced by man, serotonin can be artificially manufactured and injected into the human body when required.

THE TENDENCY TO HIDE

In certain situations, people tend to hide their true emotions. Why do they do that? Culturally, people have different responses to circumstances. In Japanese culture, people are taught from their childhood to suppress their emotions. The main reason behind this kind of practice is that being overjoyed in an environment where others are sad might arouse jealousy, anger, and even unfavorable physical reactions. This is supported by a common saying in Japan that "a nail that raises its head above the other nails risks being hammered down!" So, you will normally see Japanese acting homogenously, avoiding standing out, even if it involves not expressing one's true emotions in the public.

Apart from the cultural undertone discussed above, there are other reasons why people hide their true feelings, which include but are not limited to the following:

- Ashamed to expose personal pain, failure, and sorrow
- Not willing to appear rude or disobedient for challenging rejections, maltreatment, sexual harassment, and so on
- Unwilling to be seen as "too needy" for protesting against disaffection or not being loved by people around them
- Unable to complain against some displeasure or embarrassment so as not to appear foolish and weak
- Not willing to hurt people around them.

In fact, psychologists believe that a lot of people hide their feelings so as to remain loyal to the group, society, or community they have found themselves. Take for instance, a secretary in an office may not be willing to show anger or irritation against a boss that has abused her verbally and sexually for years, just for the purpose of not drawing the anger from her colleagues who might think she wants some financial gains from the experience or pushing to destroy the boss' image and career. The secretary may even be afraid of losing her job if her complaints are not taken seriously by the company.

Unfortunately, hiding or suppressing one's emotions has some negative effects on us. For example, people tend to be so angry and always full of resentment, because there is something or some issues burning in their hearts that they cannot divulge.

Suppressing one's emotions may have a debilitating impact on one's health. It can make your blood pressure spike or cause you to lose focus on other things you are doing for a long time. It can cause some socio-economic problems such as losing one's job, having bad relationships with people, and not being able to live a happy and peaceful life.

Manipulators usually make it difficult to express their true emotions in public. How do you expect someone who was tricked into pornography, whose naked pictures have already been taken by the manipulator to come forward and tell the whole world what he/she has been going through?

All these pieces of important information are being released to you so that you can be better armed against any hypnotist or manipulator who may want to take advantage of you or your loved ones.

II

WHAT YOU'RE UP AGAINST

3

THE PEOPLE WHO WISH TO HARM YOU

You cannot adequately protect yourself if you don't know the nature of the people that wish to harm you. The first sensible thing to do is knowing who your real enemies are. This chapter reveals the categories of people you should consider as your potential enemies and do everything within your power to avoid.

People that You Should Be Wary Of

For simplicity purposes, here is a list of ten (10) kinds of people that you should be wary of:

1. **Those who hate your guts for no apparent reason:**
   Naturally one can make enemies among colleagues, friends, and family members due to bad relationship or other reasons. However, there are some people in this life who genuinely hate you for no reason. You are neither their

business associate or partner nor share an apartment block with them; they just hate you for some reasons known only to them.

2. **Those naysayers:** Naysayers don't believe in your capabilities. They can also go out of their way to discourage others from believing in you. They spread cynical rumors about you and make others disregard your worth.

3. **People who lie about you:** In their evil minds, they fabricate lies about you and make it their business to spread calumnies about from one person to another. They instigate gullible others to treat your name disrespectfully, even though those people cannot say emphatically what you had done wrong.

4. **People who envy you too much:** There is no way you can appease someone who is quite jealous or envious of your achievements. Every time, their hearts are burning with anger that you have achieved what they would never attain in life. Even the former U.S. President, Theodore Roosevelt had this to say about envious people: *"The vice of envy is not only a dangerous, but a mean vice; for it is always a confession of inferiority. It may promote conduct which will be fruitful or wrong to others, and it must cause misery to the man who feels it."*

5. **Those who use and dump you:** You should stay away from anyone who is interested in just using and dumping you. For instance, if your business associate is only excited about using you to get new deals, but immediately shuns you after the deals have been successful, avoid such a person.

6. **People who drain all your energy:** Life is too short to hang around leeches and vampires who suck creative energy out of you. All they want to accomplish is draining you and then leaving you wimp and powerless.

7. **Bad influencer:** Most friends and partners who happen to be bad influencers in our lives are actually manipulating us for their own gains. So, why would you want to allow such discouragers to stay near you.

8. **The grumpy old friend:** Old friends are those we share the past with but, unfortunately, many of them don't deserve sharing in our present life. Why not? Grumpy old friends will be the ones to remind you how poor, unintelligent, and careless you were before. They are too engrossed in your past failures that they are not capable to appreciate your present good life or life achievements.

9. **The disloyal ones:** No matter how kind you are to disloyal people, they will eventually show their true colour—which is betraying you when you needed them the most. They are the ones who will craftily expose your dirty secrets to the whole world and come back to sympathize with you in the misery they had put you in.

10. **The Never-do-well:** This kind of person is lazy, but he/she will be the first to criticize your great work. They can never attempt to start a business, but they will come around to dissuade you from doing so.

It is clear from all indications that the different kinds of people described above can use dark psychology to take advantage or control others if they have access to it. They are likely to harm and take advantage of others when the opportunity presents itself to them.

WHY THEY DO

Manipulators and hypnotists are not just out for something, they are out to rob you of your precious time, tangible properties and, if possible, take your life in the process. The truth is that they never approach you because they have good intentions towards you. No, never. Manipulators come to you because they have some set goals they want to actualize. Hence, when they discover that they cannot naturally carry out their evil plans, they resort to using Dark Psychology to get the job done.

In recent years, some manipulators who have been apprehended and prosecuted confessed that they took Dark Psychology for the following purposes:

- To gain the upper hand in a relationship/situation
- To overpower the subconscious of their victims
- To destroy their victims' self-esteem and willpower so that they will not be able to quickly recover from their hypnotism and evil machination
- To confuse the reality of their victims while misleading them
- To take a revenge against their victims for whatever wrong they had done in the past

LET'S FACE IT

The truth is hard, and the truth is that many of our closest friends, relatives, colleagues, and neighbors are those who, on most occasions, attempt to psychologically and emotionally harm us the most.

Even the Holy Bible reckons that the most dangerous enemies people have are those of their own households.

This is why you should take this issue very seriously. Empowering yourself with the right amount of knowledge about the tricks of hypnotists and manipulators will place you ahead of them.

4

WHY DARK PSYCHOLOGY?

You probably have known why some mischievous people embrace dark psychology from the warnings already dished out in the preceding chapters. In this chapter, efforts are made to explain, in details, what constitutes a dark psychology, why it is different from the usual "psychology", the dark side of it, and why you should do everything you can to perpetually stay informed and protect yourself and your loved ones.

PSYCHOLOGY AND DARK PSYCHOLOGY, WHAT'S THE DIFFERENCE?

You should not confuse "Psychology" with "Dark Psychology". The American Psychological Association defines "Psychology" as the scientific study of mind and behavior. It is a multifaceted discipline that has been applied in various areas such as in sports, health, clinical procedures, human development, for understanding cognitive processes and social behavior.

In contrary, "Dark Psychology" can be succinctly described as the science and art of mind control and manipulation; it also studies human conditions as they relate to their psychological nature so that they can master their minds and routines for the singular purpose of preying upon others.

Even though the two types of psychology involve a scientific study of human minds and behaviors, they are so different from each other in the ways they are applied. One could differentiate one from the other by calling "Dark Psychology" a bad or negative psychology while the normal psychology as the good or positive one.

While the good psychology studies human mind so as to identify any attributes of human character that requires further development and improvement, the dark psychology analyses human mind for the purpose of discovering how it works, its apparent weaknesses, and routines in order to devise evil approaches for preying on people.

Emphasis must be laid on the differences between these two forms of psychology so that you don't mistaken one for the other. When you visit a hospital, the psychologists there are those practicing good psychology; so, you shouldn't be scared of them. On the other hand, the practitioners of dark psychology can be anywhere; they can be your relatives, friends, business associates, marketers trying to sell you something, or even your religious leaders. It takes a great deal of discernment to quickly identify these evil doers. This book is specifically written to help you spot them long before they strike and turn you into their hopeless victims.

WHY IS THERE A DARK PSYCHOLOGY?

This is an important question everyone is asking. Unfortunately, dark psychology has been in existence for centuries, even before our modern world was created. It was an ancient practice that has been adopted by people of all races, cultures, and religious affiliations. Take for example, the Jewish and Greek necromancers were early practitioners of dark psychology, invoking the spirit of the dead to manipulate the living. God, in His holiness, spoke volubly against necromancy, sorcery, casting of spells, and other detestable dark psychology practices. You can read about this in the Book of Deuteronomy 18, 9-12 (NIV): *"When you enter the land the LORD your God is giving you, do not learn to imitate the detestable ways of the nations there. 10 Let no one be found among you who sacrifices their son or daughter in the fire, who practices divination or sorcery, interprets omens, engages in witchcraft, 11 or casts spells, or who is a medium or spiritist or who consults the dead. 12 Anyone who does these things is detestable to the LORD; because of these same detestable practices the LORD your God will drive out those nations before you."*

It may interest you to know that the Book of Deuteronomy was written in 7th Century BCE when King Josiah (reigned 641-609 BCE) initiated widespread religious reforms in Jerusalem. Surprisingly, dark psychology has been in existence far before good or positive psychology came into being, it was invented around 1879 (19th

Century) when German scientist, Wilhelm Wundt set up a laboratory that was wholly dedicated to the experimental study of Psychology in Leipzig.

You are not given all these facts to scare the hell out of you; it is just an eye-opener for you to be fully aware of the long-life evil you are up against.

So, to answer this rhetorical question, "Why do people practice dark psychology?" These answers may shock you. Again, the goal is not to shock you, but to give you the unique opportunity to reassess your life and discover if you have been or will be a victim of dark psychology practitioners.

You may have probably read on the internet or heard from the others why dark psychology is being embraced by so many people and used against others. For simplicity sake, I list them by categories in this book so that you can fully grasp the extent of the wickedness perpetrated against others.

1. **Use of dark psychology in relationships:** If a guy or a lady is in any form of relationship with someone who practices dark psychology, he/she will be subjected to a number of things that do not exist in normal, loving relationships. For example, the dark psychologists will control the other partner in a way that he/she cannot refuse. The manipulator may use sex, money, mere words, and other influential things to keep the relationship going, even when the dark psychologist knows for sure that the relationship will not end as expected. You may have seen one

or some of your friends engaged with or in a relationship with a manipulator, they will just stay in the relationship for years (some are in it for up to 10 years) without any promise of marriage or common-law partnership. At the end of the day, the other person realizes that his/her time has been wasted. On a more serious note, a manipulator can push his/her boyfriend or girlfriend over the top. You will have read of people being introduced to cocaine and heroin by their lovers or conjured to borrow huge amount of money because they are so deeply in love with someone else. Those are examples of harmful effects of allowing dark psychologist into your life.

2. **Use of dark psychology in Politics:** Politicians are not only sugar-mouthed individuals who promise their electorates what they know that they can never fulfill if elected, but some of them also actually embrace dark psychology to primarily create a cult-following. A shrewd dark psychologist politician will tap into the subconsciousness of their supporters and use their grievances to make a string of incredible promises that will sweep them off their feet. Adolf Hitler came on the scene promising envious Germans that he would help them flush Jews out of their country. At that time, Jews were the most successful people in all fields; they excelled in science, business, politics, education, you name it. All those Germans needed was a country devoid of Jewish competitors. Similarly, Donald Trump presented himself to the Americans as someone who will help them drive out the Mexicans he supposedly referred

to as drug traffickers, rapists, and murderers. He captivated the Christians by promising to overturn any LGBTQ legislations that threatened American morality and strongly opposed funding abortionist organizations. Many American Christians easily fell for his manipulations without necessarily questioning Trump's personal Christian convictions as revealed in his personal life.

3. **Use of dark psychology in business:** If you are having some business dealings with a dark psychologist, it is a very dangerous thing to do. Why? His/her eyes are always on the prize—the money—and how he/she will defraud you and have everything for himself/herself. He/she doesn't mind going to any extent to actualize his/her desire. A business partner who practices dark psychology will manipulate you in every stage of your business interactions just to give himself/herself an edge in the negotiations, share of the business proceeds, or even claim everything for himself/herself. It is no longer news that the main reasons people lose in business is that the other person cheated them out of the deals. In the same way, a salesman that is nudging you into purchasing something you don't need, using weird persuasive techniques to strip you of your hard-earned money is a dark psychologist. It is not uncommon to see people regret a new purchase shortly after they had splashed the money, they didn't really want to spend on it. "Oh gosh, I shouldn't have bought this thing!" They will beat themselves soon after the dark psychologist salesperson has gone away with their money. Lately, there has been a growing concern

about corporate manipulation, whereby a company turns its employees into senseless, single-minded robots that rehearse the company's mantra every morning meeting and perceive competitors as deadly enemies. Some of these neurotic employees can leave their own families for the company, spending a lot of overtime in the office just to promote the cause of the company while not minding their own personal health and happiness.

4. **Use of dark psychology in social circles:** Everyone has friends, relatives, neighbors, or acquaintances they are very close to. Recent instances revealed that someone is likely to be manipulated 75% more times by people they trust more than those people they have no relationships with. In this case, people you confide in, such as your parents, lovers, siblings, childhood friends, and religious leaders may turn around to hurt you through selfish manipulation of your subconscious. Fake friends, they say, are worse than enemies. Their envy or jealousy of your achievements might drive them crazy to the point that they may be willing to try dark psychology on you. Are you a member of a social group or association? Have you been vilified by the other group members because one member has controlled the thoughts of the other members against you? You see, the applications of dark psychology are more prevalent than one can ever imagine.

5. **Use of dark psychology in education:** Have you ever wondered what in the world could have given birth to a very deadly movement named Islamic State in Iraq and the Levant

(ISIS) that killed many innocent souls and destabilized many erstwhile peaceful communities? That was the power of educational manipulation! Today, in various parts of the world, millions of people (or students) are still being trained to hate others for no obvious reasons. A great proportion of this educational manipulation is enshrined in religion. They coerced people to fight a "holy" religious war against people who have done nothing to incite such a holy battle. The severity of educational manipulation can be felt in every corner where violence, chaos, and societal disturbances are caused by miseducation (or misinformation), from the shores of Europe, America, to Africa.

6. **Use of dark psychology in religion:** Talking about religion is a very sensitive issue, I know. However, religion has now been used by some dastard dark psychologists as a ploy to manipulate, coerce, and rob people of their possessions. Today, church leaders, who are supposed to protect and tenderly look after congregants who look up to them for spiritual upliftment, have turned themselves into their "lords". They milk their followers of their last pound or dollar, flying in private jets while their church members grapple with disheartening levels of poverty. They have sweet-talked or manipulated their congregants into parting with the money they should have spent on themselves and their families.

You see, the outcome of the applications of dark psychology is usually the same—to leave the victim in a poorer state, more dejected, and hurt. This is why you should take every piece of information you see in this book seriously and work on keeping yourself and loved ones safe from the evil people.

THE DARK SIDE

Everyone has his/her dark side. Some people are natural liars, cheaters, and deceitful. Instead of focusing on how to rebuild or polish their characters and become good people in their respective communities, they may choose to perpetuate their asocial behaviors. What do you expect a liar to do when he/she eventually acquires the knowledge of dark psychology?

It is part of our humanity to utilize our newly acquired knowledge either to do good or evil. A doctor, for instance, knows that he/she has the power to heal or kill a patient. In this scenario, the destiny of the patient is in the doctor's hands, and if the evil part of his/her mind dictates to him/her to end the patient's life, so shall it be!

It is equally scary realizing that the proliferation of affordable dark psychology courses online can equip some fake friends, disloyal relatives, or even envious colleagues with some powers to manipulate you. When a dark psychologist pounces on you, he/she doesn't have any good thoughts or intentions towards you. All he/she wants to accomplish is to bring you down, take your possessions and, in an unfortunate circumstance, take your life. To be sincere, we are in more danger right now than ever before; this is why it is advisable you should acquire all the necessary knowledge about these evil people and protect yourself.

BE WARY

It is now your responsibility to be wary of people that may want to use dark psychology against you and your loved ones. Protecting your sanity and living a balanced, happy life should be the goal you daily pursue, because those great things you cherish, such as your peace of mind, happiness, and balanced life are what dark psychologists are targeting.

You probably have read or heard people say any of these things:

- Simple manipulation is not dark psychology
- Hypnotism is not dark psychology
- Coercive persuasion is not dark psychology
- Simple mind control is not dark psychology
- Neuro-linguistic programming (NLP) is not dark psychology

Be careful, the first subtle action of a manipulator is to misinform you. Those who are clamoring that simple manipulation, hypnotism, coercive persuasion, mind control, and NLP aren't elements of dark psychology have grossly missed the point. In Science Daily, a reputable publication that provides current information about how pure science affects humanity, has this to say about "dark psychology": *"All dark traits can be traced back to the general tendency of placing one's own goals and interests over those of others even to the extent of taking pleasure in hurting other's -- along with a host of beliefs that serve as justifications and thus prevent feelings of guilt, shame, or the like."*

If someone will use simple manipulation, NLP, or coercive persuasion to make himself/herself better at your expense, that counts as dark psychology because the person does not need your permission to psychologically manipulate you so that he/she can get away with whatever he/she wants, justifying his/her actions with certain beliefs.

As you continue reading this book and unearthing more facts about dark psychologists and their evil tricks, something that should be ringing at the back of your mind should be: "Only I am responsible for protecting myself!". Before you open the doors of your mind to someone, asking these six questions may help you stay safe:

- **Who is this person?** Ask yourself who this person is: What kind of character does he/she have? What is appealing about him/her? Is he the kind of person I can confidently open up to? These preliminary questions will help you discover what kind of person you are about to allow into your space. Character, they say, is like a smoke; there is no way anyone can hide his/her character for a very long time. Like smoke, even when it is covered with a bowl, it will find a way to make itself known. And when you discovered that a person's character doesn't match with yours, and that there is no inkling or chemistry between the two of you, it is a sign that you should literally take cover. Do not be that person who believes he/she can change someone. The only person that will be changed, that will be decimated in an event of manipulation is you, if you are not careful.
- **What does he/she want?** Sometimes people hide their true motives when they approach us for something. A

person who presents himself/herself as prospective business partner may actually be looking for love. You can save yourself from a lot of embarrassment if you could quickly detect what an acquaintance truly wants before letting your guards down on all fronts. You can proactively protect yourself in every area of your life.

- **How much space can I give to him/her?** Not everyone that knocks on the door of your mind should be welcomed in. Some people deserve to have doors slammed shut in their faces, because of the extent of their wickedness. Great and talented entertainers have lost their dear lives because they were not careful who they allowed into their personal spaces. Without mentioning names, beautiful singers who took to taking drugs and energetic sportsmen and sportswomen whose careers got destroyed before their lovers had introduced them to enhancing drugs. Had they been careful about who they allowed into their private spaces; they would still be alive today making good music.

- **How to act when I discover early signs of manipulation:** If you detect early on that the person you are dealing with is a manipulator, count yourself very lucky. The truth is that most victims don't even know they are already in the trap of a dark psychologist until he/she has finished dealing with them. So, after discovering he/she is a manipulator, you have to act swiftly. If you can, sit the dark psychologist down and question his/her motives. However, if you sense he/she could be defensive to the point of being violent, you can easily let him/her go without raising any dust. Just cut off your engagement with him/her.

- **What am I gaining from this?** For anyone who has already gone too deep with a manipulator or dark psychologist, there is still a way to escape. It begins by asking this question: "What am I gaining from this?" Is this situation comfortable for my personal and professional development? Take for instance, if you have married a manipulator or signed a multiyear contract with a manipulating company or business associate, you still need to ask yourself whether you are deriving any tangible thing from the alliance or not. If you are just being used on a daily and you have nothing to show for being in that relationship, it is time to consider the next question.

- **How do I get myself out of this mess?** Very few victims of dark psychology practitioners get to this stage where they can quickly come to their senses and strategize to free themselves from a manipulator's stranglehold. Many of them have already been decimated, abused, used, harassed, and pushed into a complete state of hopelessness before they can recoil from their misery streak. If you are in the situation, you should immediately seek help; it may be difficult for you to take yourself out of the funk you have put yourself. You should consider yourself fortunate to still be alive to rehabilitate yourself. Many have been sent to their graves early; they are no more here to reflect on the mess they have made of their lives by carelessly allowing manipulators to destroy them.

One of the reasons this book was written is to create enough awareness for people so that they don't necessarily fall into all the problems that manipulations, dark psychology, and hypnotism bring about. You can save your friends, families, and colleagues by sharing all that you will discover in this book with them.

Being a victim of a dark psychologist is never pretty: Apart from the financial and social fallouts from the experience, it could lead to a disgraceful mental health issue. For the rest of their lives, the victims of dark psychology often find it difficult to trust anyone; they are always suspicious of people's actions because they cannot afford to be maltreated again. They naturally fortify their defense mechanisms and keep potential manipulators at bay.

Are you wondering why practitioners of dark psychologists don't seem to have any conscience that their actions are hurting others? In the next chapter, you will discover the three main or core dark traits in people who derive some satisfaction in causing discomfort for others.

In their research, Ingo Zettler, Professor of Psychology at the University of Copenhagen, and two German colleagues, Morten Moshagen from Ulm University and Benjamin E. Hilbig from the University of Koblenz-Landau concluded that *"in the same way, the dark aspects of human personality also have a common denominator, which means that -- similar to intelligence -- one can say that they are all an expression of the same dispositional tendency."*

This indicates that whether they are hypnotists or manipulators, their evil goals are the same—to turn people into hopeless beings!

5

THE DARK TRIAD

The dark sides of humanity, or to put it mildly, the dark behaviors of human beings through which they inflict pain and sorrow on others, come in different forms. In this book, attempt is made to distil all those various acts of human wickedness into just three major types. Collectively, they are referred to as "The Dark Triad".

WHAT IS THE DARK TRIAD?

The Dark Triad is not a phrase you often hear people throw around, but they describe some of the major psychological traits exhibited by people. These traits dictate how people behave, and how they treat the others in their surroundings.

History has it that the term "The Dark Triad" started to gain public recognition in 1990s when a group of psychologists/scientists including McHoskey, Worzei, Szyarto, and Delroy L. Paulhus debated the similarities and differences among the three core components of The Dark Triad, namely, Narcissism, Machiavellianism, and Psychopathy.

Since then, the term has garnered much interest among psychologists/scientists, and studies and/or experiments on how it fully impacts humanity.

NARCISSISM

Narcissism originates from a Greek mythology that tells the story of a hunter, Narcissus, who got attracted to or fell in love with his own shadow in the pool until he drowned. A narcissistic person has a tendency to exhibit any or most of the following personality traits: Pride, lack of empathy, egotism, arrogance, boastfulness, grandiosity, hypersensitive to criticism, and selfishness.

It is human nature to always desire to be in relationship or have something to do with whoever agrees with us on most occasions. If you are working with or in a romantic relationship with a narcissist, you will feel some degree of discomfort.

There are four distinct dimensions of narcissism observable in various capacities:

- **Leadership/Authority:** Narcissistic leaders demonstrate absolute disregard for their subordinates. Do you know those self-assured company owners or presidents who look down on every other person on their premises? They are only concerned about what they can gain from their employees, pushing them so hard to the point that it may be to their detriment. But then they never cared a hoot about their employees' welfare.

- **Superiority/Arrogance:** Some people who fortunately found themselves in high, covetous social positions or have luckily acquired some wealth may be so arrogant to the point of being cruel. He/she will reveal his sense of superiority to everyone around him/her, making them feel inferior at all times.

- **Self-absorption/Self-admiration:** Dealing with self-absorbed or self-admired persons is the most difficult thing to do. They only see the good in themselves; every other person, to them, is useless, hopeless, and not worth appreciating.

- **Exploitativeness/entitlement:** If you are in a relationship of any sort with an exploitative individual, he/she takes from you to make himself/herself better. In other words, they add value to themselves by reducing you. A husband/wife who often feels entitled will drive you crazy until he/she gets exactly what he/she wants. Come to think of spending thirty or forty years with people like that, you will both be physically and mentally exhausted.

Why narcissists are very dangerous

Depending on which culture you are coming from, sometimes the societies or cultures confuse narcissism with high self-esteem. They do not necessarily see it as psychological or behavioural disorder. This wrong perception of narcissism gives ample room for narcissists to go out of control. There has been reports of narcissistic abuse lately due to the fact that our cultures—most especially, the winner-takes-all mentality, has given some people an edge to undermine the integrity of the others while claiming they are more important that anyone else.

Another disturbing issue is what psychologists refer to as narcissistic rage, which often occurs when someone who feels too important discovers that people around him/her aren't buying into their assumed self-importance. Many people have ended up being maltreated or suffered what is called narcissistic injury because the narcissists think they have the right to defend themselves, or whatever they believe about themselves.

It must be stated clearly that no one who inhabits the same space with a narcissist will ever like what he/she is experiencing. In certain extreme circumstances, it may cause their victims to suffer mental health issues—just like an abusing wife or husband will cause their spouse to go through some moments of insanity.

Three main approaches often used by a narcissistic individual to remain relevant in his/her own eyes is to manipulate others through:

- **Threats:** They can threaten to do some harsh things to anyone who are not on the same page with them.
- **Guilt:** They make others feel guilty or less important in all conditions.
- **Jealousy/envy:** Presenting themselves as the most

successful person in the room, thereby spurring people into becoming envious or jealous.

MACHIAVELLIANISM

The word "Machiavellianism" is coined from the name of a 16th-century Italian politician or diplomat, Niccolo Machiavelli. He published a book in 1513 titled "The Prince" which was seen by his readers as a shameful endorsement of the tricky dark arts of manipulating people with deceitfulness and exhibiting unempathetic temperament.

Psychologists have since labelled this trait after him, and a Machiavellian individual employs lies, tricks, and duplication to get whatever he/she wants. He/she does so with apparent lack of emotion. He/she hotly pursues his/her self-interest at the expense of others and lack morality.

If you have ever come across someone in your life who will do anything, including lying and being dubious just to get whatever he/she is aiming at, you have dealt with a Machiavellian person.

It is an undeniable fact that everyone is different. To have a better understanding of how a Machiavellian person thinks, feels, and reasons, we need to consider these attitudes that are usually attributed to Machiavellianism:

- **Poor emotional attachment to others:**
  Machiavellianism is characterized by extremely cold disposition towards others. In other words, they do not, in

principle, express empathy towards anyone; when someone is in pain or enmeshed in some dangerous circumstances, a Machiavellian person just looks the other way instead of showing some sympathy. This explains why they are easily susceptible to harming other people without showing any remorse.

- **Deceitful manipulation:** Even though a Machiavellian individual realizes that he/she doesn't deserve something, he/she will still give it a shot and use lies, tricks, and deceits to take advantage of others. This is common in business, politics, diplomacy, and even among siblings.

- **Duplicity:** Duplicity entails calling things what they are not in order to flatter and deceive people at the same time. A person that shows duplicity in all his/her dealings is likely to use sweet words to cajole people, causing them to do what they didn't intend to do or part with their money or other valuable possessions. This attribute is common to all manipulators whose primary intentions are to make themselves better at the expense of others. They can praise and confuse you with their fake interest in your wellbeing; however, they are not being truthful because down in their hearts, they know that they do not care a hoot about you. Isn't this dangerous?

- **Hardcore selfishness:** By default, it is practically impossible for a Machiavellian to put himself/herself in the position of his/her victim. In other words, they don't seem to feel the same level of pain and agony that their unlucky victims are going through. This leaves them with only one option—to concentrate fully on what they could gain from a relationship. This hardcore selfishness is what motivates a Machiavellian individual to push others to the wall while enjoying himself/herself throughout the entire process. Naturally, friendship between two people is expected to be based on mutual self-respect and considerations. However, when one of them is a shameless and heartless Oliver Twist, asking for more and more until the other is exhausted and dried up, such a friend must be avoided at all cost.

- **Irresistible hunger for power and relevance:**
  Excessive greed and personal gratification are two things that often motivate a Machiavellian in any relationship. They may first pretend as if money, power, and personal aggrandizements are not their primary goals for striking up an acquaintance with you, but their barefaced pretentions won't last long. The eagerness with which they pursue their selfish desires can be harmful as they aren't willing to slow down until they accomplish their evil intentions. This is why you should take flight when you come across such an individual.

PSYCHOPATHY

Psychopathy is the third of The Dark Triad, and it is considered, in psychiatry, as antisocial personality disorder (ASPD). The word "psychopathy" is usually confused with sociopathy and psychosis. Sociopathy is used to describe a list of asocial behaviors that include manipulation, lack of manners and empathy, aggressiveness, and deitfulness. On the other hand, psychosis is a condition, usually associated with mental illness, that affects the way a person's brain processes information. A psychotic individual may lose touch with reality, and he/she may be seeing, hearing, believing things that are not real.

Signs of Psychopathy

A psychopath usually shows some or all of the following signs:

- **Asocial behavior:** A psychopath often reveals some asocial behaviors which indicate a certain degree of irresponsibility on his/her part. He/she may be aggressive to others and show a low moral sense.
- **Absolute disregard for the rights of others:** Psychopaths may find it very difficult to appreciate the fact that others have rights that should be protected and respected.
- **Right versus the wrong:** Owing to their callousness, psychopaths may not be able to differentiate the right from the wrong. When they are hurting people, they do not perceive it as a bad thing. In fact, they derive some weird joy in putting others in trouble. More so, what seems right to them might only be things that tickle their fancy, even though they are publicly considered to be illegal or immoral.
- **Apparent lack of empathy:** Psychopaths are not necessarily empathetic to other people's feelings, whether they are sad or in pain. This accounts for their cruel attitudes towards others.

- **Habitual liars:** On most occasions, psychopaths are liars or have a tendency to lie often. They need to fabricate falsehood from time to time to cover up their selfish behaviors. They never care if their lies could put others in a big problem or not; all they want is to achieve their self-centered goals.

- **Cruelly manipulating and hurting others:** It has become psychopaths' second nature to manipulate and hurt others. They do this both randomly and intentionally. And they do not care what effects their unkind actions would have on others. Can you imagine how annoying it will be when someone who causes you pain does not feel he/she is doing a bad thing.

- **Tendency to break laws:** It is common for psychopaths to have recurring problems with the law. It is in their attitude to disrespect law and order. In addition to undermining other people's rights, they go out of their ways to flout rules and laws enacted for safety in the societies. You are likely going to see a psychopath driving on the wrong side of the road or smoking in non-smoking areas.

- **Common disregard towards responsibility:** Since they have low moral sense, they do not show adequate regard toward any act of responsibility. Psychopaths are much likely not to pay their taxes or participate in community development activities.

- **Reckless behavior:** They act recklessly and show no respect for people in places of authority. They can easily join criminal gangs or groups of domestic terrorists. They can act impetuously in the public, like driving a car through a crowd.

- **Tendency to take risks:** Psychopaths are known for taking risks. Sometimes their risky actions expose others to danger, and they do not really care about the outcomes of their deeds.

Similarities and differences among the Dark Triads

The main similarity among the Dark Triads is that a Narcissist, a Machiavellian, and a Psychopath lack empathy for others' feelings. They are not concerned about how their hurtful actions will impact the lives of their victims. This lackadaisical demonstration of wickedness is why people generally dislike them. You cannot afford to stay in a long relationship with any of them because it will have some effects on your mental health. All of them are also shameless manipulators; they are naturally fond of deceiving others to achieve their selfish ambitions.

However, while a Narcissist is boastful and full of pride, a Machiavellian lacks moral aptitude and practices duplicity, and a Psychopath demonstrates absolute disregard for the rights of others and under risky and illegal activities that can endanger others' lives.

As you can see, those who habitually exhibit the characteristics of the Dark Triads have no reasons to care about you. They really can't understand whether what they are doing to you is hurtful or not. They do not show empathy; in short, they are not feeling what you feel. And that is why you should protect yourself and your loved ones from them.

6

HARMLESS PERSUASION VERSUS DARK PERSUASION

How do you differentiate a harmless salesperson that knocks on your door to sell you something that you probably need from the one who intentionally comes to your home to carry out dark persuasion on you? Most people will agree that this is a very tricky question. It is an undeniable fact that we are regularly subjected to these two kinds of persuasion: Harmless persuasion and dark persuasion.

In this chapter, you will discover some elements of dark persuasion and red flags you should always be looking for when approached by someone who displays some traits of persuasive manipulation.

PERSUASION, AT ITS CORE

Persuasion is the process of compulsively passing certain information across to someone whose attitude may be altered or influenced by the information delivered. In itself, persuasion doesn't connote negativism; it is not harmful since the person who is being persuaded has the right to accept or reject the information or persuasion.

In life, persuasion is a common tool used by people for different good purposes. It can be used to engender an effective communication within a team in an organization. Parents normally persuade their children to choose the right paths in life. Teachers often persuade their students to do their best at their examinations.

However, some psychologists believe that persuasive communication, though commonly employed in education and meetings, may turn out to be forceful and threatening. Take for instance, a teacher may choose to punish one of his/her students by talking down to him/her. This kind of punitive approach may elicit negative reactions from the student being targeted. The student may be scared, ashamed, and defensive, having been embarrassed in front of the entire class.

In principle, the nature of a persuasive communication depends on how the receiver of the information interprets it. Take for example, while Student A, shy and unassuming may consider being talked down in front of class as demeaning and improper, Student B, popular and shameless, may capitalize on the teacher's action to become more popular with his classmates.

WHEN IS IT CONSIDERED HARMLESS?

As briefly hinted above, persuasion may be harmless and good for the receiver. Why? Because not all persuasive communications are meant to harass, demean, and manipulate the receiver, as shown below. We can see examples of this in marketing, literature, legal practice, and even in all professions.

- **Harmless persuasion in marketing:** From the fleeting commercial adverts on your TVs to long, windy infomercials, some companies located somewhere are bombarding you with persuasive information to encourage you to dip your hands in your wallet or purse and buy something from them. Whether they appear at your doorstep physically or reach out to you via email or web chat, salespersons are trying to convince you to intentionally part with some of your money and purchase some things from them. As you can see, it is done harmlessly: No threatening words are used, no one is beating fear into you for the purpose of destabilizing you emotionally. There are reports that some overambitious salespersons do go beyond the sensible marketing stint, pulling some little persuasive tricks on you. However, if you are able to quickly come to your senses, you can tell such an overreaching salesperson to stop it, and he/she will immediately behave properly. He/she may even apologize for pushing too hard. It is clear that such a salesperson, despite being anxious to sell his/her merchandizes, doesn't mean evil for his/her prospective customer. He/she will do everything in his/her power to act nicely and courteously.

- **Harmless use of persuasion in literature:** There are some aspects of literature that require students to persuasively defend their beliefs in reading and writing critique classes. Each student will vehemently speak in support of their personal opinions or perspectives about the book being read or a writing piece under critique. None of them is making an attempt to manipulate anyone; they are just engaging one another in an academic persuasion.

- **Harmless application of persuasion in legal proceedings:** Anyone who has attended a legal proceeding at the court will have seen how lawyers compellingly persuade the judges to consider the case from their perspectives. The lawyers, doing their job, do not mean any evil for the judges; they are merely doing what they needed to do for the goodness of their clients. Persuasion, in such a light, is positive and harmless.

- **Harmless persuasions in other areas:** Everyone will agree that physicians, sometimes and allowed by their profession, do persuade their patients to take some medicines or try a new type of treatment. In the same way, when a police officer persuades a criminal to surrender himself/herself to the law, the officer doesn't mean to harm the criminal at that moment if he/she doesn't make any threatening gestures towards the officer. If you are a fan of football, you will also have seen how coaches yell at their players on the field, persuading to tackle an advancing opponent ruthlessly but skillfully. In all these rife examples, no one is at danger of being dangerously manipulated, undermined, and turned into a victim.

You may be wondering why politicians' speeches are not used as a typical example of positive persuasive communication. While it may be true that not all politicians make conscious efforts to manipulate their followers or party members, however, politicians' tendency to incite crowd against their political rivals makes it unsuitable to consider their speeches harmless or non-insinuating. In politics, it is usually "I" against "He/she" or "Us" against "Them". This can establish a negative atmosphere whereby members of a political party can cause mayhem that could lead to unprecedented destruction and harm for members of the opposing party.

Religious leaders, for example, are good examples of people that adopt persuasive communication to exhort their followers to remain holy and steadfast in their religious callings. They may shout at the top of their lungs at the altars just to make sure that their congregants aren't backsliding, leaving their faith in the Lord to engage in sinful life.

Positive, harmless persuasion is meant to bring the best out of someone else's life. It is a tool for nudging people to take decisive actions in making their lives better.

Elements of harmless persuasion

For simplicity purpose, these are characteristics of harmless persuasion that you should be looking for. Being vigilant on all occasions can save you and your loved ones from impending calamities. When someone is persuading you for any reasons at all, see if he/she is:

- **Putting your needs forward:** A good salesperson will repeatedly tell you what you can gain from purchasing his/her products or services. Your parents, who disturb you with their countless pieces of advice, sometimes unsolicited, are just rooting for you and your future success. Your teacher who seems to be talking to you harshly in front of other classmates is trying his/her best to guide you. You see, you are at the center of a positive, harmless persuasion, geared towards making you better and stronger.

- **Establishing harmless relationships:** Cruel manipulators don't necessarily care about making you feel welcomed or appreciated in their space. They abruptly come into your life, want to control you, and then leave you dejected and spent after they might have achieved their selfish ambitions. Isn't it crazy for a hopeless guy who slithers his way into a celebrity lady's bedroom only to hold her to ransom, threatening to release all her nude pictures on the internet if she doesn't pay some undisclosed amount of money? Immediately you noticed a sneaky person trying to control you even if you have just met a few days, weeks, months ago, you should consider that as a red flag. It is important to draw a comparison with that; a well-intentioned person will come to your life, tread carefully based on your permission, and continue to hold you in high esteem. Nowadays, the internet has made it possible for people to fall in love without getting to knowing each other better. There have been confirmable reports that some unlucky girls have fallen into the hands of serial killers or pedophiles because they were not quite cautious enough in their approach to seeking friendships from strangers.

- **Listening to your opinions:** if anyone trying to persuade you for whatever reasons fails to listen to your own opinions on the situation, there is every possibility that such a person may be undermining your personal rights. That should give you a sign that the person you are dealing with has a tendency of being a manipulator. Even strict parents tend to give their children the benefit of the doubt to prove themselves nowadays. For every persuasion you received, it is in your hands to accept or reject it. So, if anyone, it doesn't matter who he/she, is compelling or coercing you to do what you dislike, that is purely a manipulative act.

WHAT MAKES IT DARK?

At this junction you may be wondering what exactly counts as dark persuasions, and what makes them dark? Efforts are made in this book to simplify everything for you. So, sit down and let each fact sink into your mind.

Persuasion becomes dark when these dark persuasion techniques are used by manipulators to steal from you, control you, or compel you to choose a dangerous course of life. Anyone who utilizes any of the following dark persuasion techniques on you is not worth your time and respect:

- **Seduction:** Literally, the word "seduction" means the act of persuading someone of the opposite sex to go to bed with you. While this definition is directly related to the issue of manipulation, whereby men and women use "sex" as a weapon to control one another. However, "seduction" has expanded meanings—it could mean the act of luring someone into believing something so that they take actions without properly thinking it through. The creators of Ponzi schemes apply this interpretation to rob people of their hard-earned wealth. They will tell you to deposit your money in their schemes and earn multiple interests in returns. If your country's harmonized interest rate is around 15%, a Ponzi Scheme may be promising you an interest of 35% on any deposit you made. True to their words, the Ponzi schemers will pay you the promised 35% in the first few months of depositing your hard-earned money in their coffers. However, after some time, having collected a lot of money from different victims, the schemers will turn their backs on everyone and declare bankruptcy, while hiding their loots in foreign bank accounts abroad.

- **Brainwashing:** Brainwashing, which is also known as coercive persuasion, is broadly discussed in Chapter 8 of this book. It is a common dark persuasive technique used by dogmatic religious, political, and cultural leaders. They forcefully put "thoughts" into their followers' heads and rob them the unique opportunity to think for themselves. Hitler did it perfectly and pulled the entire world through a six-year war. Several terrorist organizations are employing the same technique to turn their followers into "human" explosives that wear self-detonating bombs and kill innocent people.

- **Enticement:** A manipulator may decide to first entice his/her prospective victim with something he/she cannot resist or refuse. An unemployed lady may be trapped by a job offer that does not exist. People have been ensnared by fraudsters who presented irresistible financial investments to them, only for them to lose all their money invested in the spurious or fake investments.

- **Coercion:** This is entirely different from the other methods adopted by manipulators in the sense that it is the person controlling them—a spouse, relation, or business partner— forces them to do the exact opposite they intended to do. When held hostage by a kidnapper, the victim is bound to follow all the strict instructions passed down by his/her captor. In this scenario, there is little chance to oppose the kidnapper that could be very dangerous.

- **Isolationism:** In certain cases, a manipulator may stay in the background and direct others under his/her guidance to carry out his/her dark persuasive communication. Those acting under his leadership will then bombard the targeted victim with whatever actions they are directed to undertake. If the victim fails to cower or surrender, they will isolate him/her from their group or association. In this way, they are trying to make the victim suffer from guilt that was projected on him/her by others. In very few circumstances, the targeted victim will be able to free himself/herself from their attacks, which could be prolonged.

In summary, a manipulator is a self-centered, malicious individual whose primary aim is to control, coerce, decimate, and exterminate his/her victim if he/she is left unchallenged.

DIFFERENTIATING THE TERMS

It is important to identify the similarities and differences between persuasion and manipulation. This will remove any confusion that often arises when people use the two terms. While they do have some similarities, they are quite different from one another.

Similarities: Both persuasion and manipulation involve talking or have some discussions with another person. And both persuasion and manipulation are initiated by the individual who is trying to persuade or manipulate the other.

Major differences: The differences between persuasion and manipulation can be best understood by considering the three points highlighted below:

- **The intention:** People are usually persuaded to embrace a better way of life or turn away from bad lifestyles that could harm them and destroy their future. A child that keeps failing his/her exams may receive constructive persuasion from his/her concerned teacher. On the contrary, manipulation is intended to turn the receiver into a victim of the manipulator, for the purpose of robbing him/her of some precious things.
- **Truthfulness:** When you receive persuasion from someone who truly cares about your wellbeing or success, he/she will interact with you in all honesty and truthfulness. He/she will frankly address the main issue that may be threatening your career, marriage, or success.

However, a manipulator comes to you with all tools in his/her pocket. If he/she discovers that you are a hard nut to crack, the manipulator will employ falsehood or blatant lies to confuse and mislead you. A Ponzi Scheme owner will tell you all manners of lies just to make sure you part with your hard-earned money and invest it in his/her Scheme.

- **Who benefits from the interaction?** It is obvious that constructive or positive persuasion is meant to encourage you to veer from a wrong path to a much promising career choice or lifestyle. On the other hand, a manipulator comes after you because of what he/she stand to gain from the relationship or interaction. In this scenario, the manipulator will make himself/herself the center or focus of the interaction instead of you.

- **The approach adopted:** Persuasion is mostly soft and benign; there are no overt issuance of threats and acrimonious words or expressions. However, a lot of threats and coercion are employed in manipulation. The goal of a shameless manipulator is to beat fear into the heart of his/her victim before decimating them. Most people lose their mental strength when bullied or threatened; that is exactly the approach manipulators use.

KNOW WHAT IT IS

You should be aware of these persuasion techniques so that you can immediately detect when people go overboard while using any of them. Manipulators also use them, but they always stretch things too thin just to make sure that they achieve their evil intentions:

- **Anticipation:** When you are being persuaded, what the person who is persuading you wants to achieve is to make you anticipate the good things that may come to your life if you choose to change course and do the right things in your education, business, marriage, and so on. A picture of a better life will be painted for you to fantasize about and work towards attaining.

- **Unity of purpose:** The person persuading you will make you feel that you are on the same page—that there is unity of purpose between the two of you. Take for example, if you want to advance in your business and increase your stream of income, a mentor will let you understand that he/she is there for you so that you can improve your cash flow. At that moment, the person isn't talking about himself/herself, he/she is discussing how you can take your business to the next level.

- **Emotional energy:** Everyone loves it when friends, relatives, and neighbors demonstrate strong interest in their well-being, because they will reveal their feelings towards us through their high-energy emotional expressions. Imagine you have just won the lottery, and a neighbor runs out of his/her flat to greet you on the street with two arms stretched out in from of him//her. That shows the level of excitement in him/her to see you succeed!

- **Commitment and consistency:** Naturally, we tend to

listen to someone who consistently commits himself/herself to directing us in the right ways. We will feel that they have abandoned their own needs to concentrate on making us happier, better, and more prosperous. To be honest, that is one of the best approaches for persuading someone—sticking with it until success comes.

- **"Because..."**: Everyone desires to know the reason why he/she is being persuaded. In that case, an individual who thinks that there are cogent reasons you should change courses and embrace another approach will come to tell you the reasons why. He/she may be your colleague, boss, classmate, or even your spouse. Knowing the reasons for a change might speed up the process of adapting to a newer or more improved system.

- **Reasoning by analogy:** It is common for people to reason by analogy when persuading one another. They can use stories, anecdotes, past testimonies, and popular events to drive home their points. This seems to have much impact on the person being persuaded. They can see clearly that someone was in their position before he/she did something to get out of the hopeless situation. Poor people are persuaded to work harder; telling them the story of people who have got out of poverty through sheer hard work may serve a great motivator.

- **Reciprocity:** Sometimes you are persuaded to take a certain action based on the good thing you have done for someone in the past. The person is merely reciprocating the good gesture by asking you to do the same thing. If you have, by chance, asked a friend to pay a lottery. If your friend surprisingly wins, he/she will surely come around to advise you to try it, too.

- **Authority:** An individual may offer you some pieces of advice based on his/her experience in the same area or field. His/her authority in the matter under discussion is enough to add more weight to his/her persuasion.

- **Urgency:** You can be persuaded by an individual who lets you see the urgency of the issue at hand, and that you have got no time to waste on rejecting his/her advice. In this case, you are encouraged to consider the matter quickly and make a sensible decision on time.

Warning: As harmless as the techniques outlined above are, be forewarned that manipulators can also utilize them to hurt you. It is up to you to use your discretion in detecting when tricky people are asking for more than you could give. That could be a timely signal that a manipulator has invaded your space. Be wise!

7

WHAT YOU NEED TO KNOW ON MANIPULATION

People often confuse psychological manipulation with emotional manipulation. Even though the two terms share certain similarities, they are quite different from each other. Psychological manipulation is a kind of social influence on a person or a group of people so as to change their behaviors or perceptions about things through deceptive, indirect, or hidden tactics. However, emotional manipulation occurs when someone, for selfish purposes, tries to control others through exploitative strategies so that he/she can decimate, coerce, and even victimize his/her targets. These kinds of manipulation involve both targeting a victim, but emotional manipulation carries more weight than psychological.

Watch out: Most of the people that use emotional manipulation on us are those that are very close to us— our lovers, relatives, best friends, and colleagues!

THE MANIPULATIVE BEHAVIOR

People are often advised to look out for some manipulative behaviors in people around them. The most important question that normally comes up is: What makes some people be manipulative in their behaviors or attitudes?

There are three unique answers to that question:

1. **Hereditary reason:** A person can come from a lineage or family history that literally has the "genes" for manipulating others. In other words, they naturally exhibit attitudes that redolent with dishonesty and lies. There could be a very strong reason for displaying this kind of behavior. If the family had in the past struggled for power, material resources, love and affection, control, social status and acceptance, it could have shifted their brains towards adapting several deceptive tactics to get by. This struggle might have occurred within the family or with an outsider. As a result of this, to keep whatever they had gained from deceptions, or manipulating others, they will persist in their socially unacceptable ways. Haven't you ever heard of an expression that "deception runs deep in that family!" It means everyone, from their young to old ones are shameless liars. There are many families like that, most especially the political families. They could be rude, deceitful, and manipulative just to keep maintaining their current social status.

2. **Not properly developed during the formative**

years: Those who did not grow up properly during their formative years often displayed certain cognitive weaknesses in their behaviors. And to make up for their shortcomings, they can be strangely aggressive, manipulative, and inconsiderate. It is their natural defense mechanisms; sometimes, they cannot personally explain some of their attitudes because they have become part and parcel of their daily routines. Therefore, they may not have room to accommodate feelings for others nor empathize with them. All they want is to prove to everyone that they are culturally, economically, socially, and professionally perfect, even though there is evidence about them that proves otherwise.

3. **Supportive environments for manipulation:**
   Sometimes, people don't want to be manipulative; however, the environments where they live allow such a thing. So, since it has become a norm or trend within that jurisdiction to be cunning, exploitative, deceptive, inconsiderate, aggressive, and manipulating, it just becomes a status quo for everyone there. In a competitive environment, such as a workplace or an industry, people or business owners tend to compete dangerously with one another. If there are not rules or standards that forbid or discourage unfair practices, there could be chronic manipulations in such an environment. To stay on top of their games, people could be ruthless, malicious, and manipulative.

ARE YOU BEING MANIPULATED?

Unfortunately, not everyone can consciously detect or know that they are being manipulated. This may be due to the fact that they are living in an environment where acts of manipulation are rife or tolerated; so, they wrongly perceive manipulation as one of the social behaviors in their vicinities. Scientists and psychologists have spent years studying or researching how people can easily detect that a manipulator has entered into their space. Most studies reveal that people could only feel the effects of manipulation; that is when it dawns on them that they have become victims of cruel manipulations.

If you are experiencing any of the feelings outlined below, chances are that you are being manipulated by someone you allowed into your life:

- **Feeling being monitored:** If your instinct tells you that you are being constantly monitored, maybe by a jealous lover, an overbearing parent, or boss, you are inadvertently becoming a victim of manipulation. Those who are monitoring you have only one goal in mind: To dominate or control you! This is quite frustrating because you do not call for this kind of monitoring, and hence you cannot do anything to cause the evil monitoring to cease. You should take action immediately when you discover this: You may challenge those undertaking the monitoring or do something that will frustrate their weird efforts.
- **You are constantly being objectified:** Instead of being respected and treated nicely by people around you, they

pretty much treat you like an object. You are perceived as a "sex object" or any other types of objectification. In romantic relationships, you may be tolerated simply because of what your partner or spouse is deriving from you. In psychology, this condition is referred to "object constancy". Instead of openly showing their hatred, distaste, and anger towards you, they will continue to bear you as long as you continue to tickle their objectification fantasy. Trouble will begin when you no longer fit the bill. Reports show that many couples who were happy immediately after their weddings will start to have some problems in their marriage as soon as the wives began to give birth to children. You know what, since the women could no longer be referred to as "sexy", their unsatiated husbands will start looking for other pretty ladies outside, engaging in extramarital affairs. In essence, people who objectify you don't naturally love you; they are just putting up with you as long as you are satisfying their fantasies. In the same way, an inconsiderate, narcissistic employer may not like you at all; what he/she cares about is the good job you are doing for his/her business.

- **The need to feel superior:** Manipulators do not only target weak or vulnerable people, but they also have the habit of hunting for strong and emotionally stable individuals they can decimate. They realize that destroying a powerful person is a good opportunity to show that they matter. Their Machiavellian spirit will not rest until they have brought a highly placed individual down. If someone is always after you at your place of work or meetings, castigating you openly in the presence of other colleagues, you should mark such a person. He/she is trying to manipulate you and control your thoughts. In politics, the primary goal of an opposition politician is to make you lose focus, diverting your attention from your great policies while spending most of your precious time to respond to their destabilizing tactics.

- **Projection:** After spending some time to study you, manipulators will know what to do to get you angry or to be emotionally disturbed. To make the matter worse, they will turn around and accuse you of doing what they are exactly doing, deceptively covering their actions. For example, a manipulator may wrongly allege that you are planning to criminally implicate him/her at work. Meanwhile, his/her daily actions are to ensnare you at work by fabricating some lies against you. If you are not careful, you may believe their projections and start absorbing wrong energies.

- **Gaslighting:** The word "gaslighting" came from a 1944 movie "Gaslight" where an actor was controlling his wife and made her believe that she was crazy. In the same way, a manipulator nowadays will want to control or overpower you by letting you feel like you are crazy, literally. They will make you feel bad about yourself and position themselves as the solutions you need to be free from your problems. In that case, if you allow them, you have given them a front-seat position in your life; they can control your life the way they like.

- **Perspecticide:** This is a kind of emotional abuse that

occurs in a relationship whereby one partner controls the other to the extent that the victim loses his/her grip on truth and self-consciousness. The victim in this relationship automatically becomes a prisoner in that scenario, having lost his/her senses and cannot stand for what he/she believes. The controlling partner is responsible for everything, including what social, religious, and cultural ideas they must embrace in the relationship.

- **Bonding through trauma:** Manipulators are not always downright harsh and unkind. Sometimes, they act nicely to their victims. This is why some victims in abusive relationships never felt the urge to leave; they enjoy the feeling of being catered for but grossly overlooked the maltreatment they are getting from their manipulating partners.

- **"You are not doing your part":** When in a condition of psychological abuse, the controlling partner will always make the other feel inadequate in everything. He/she will usually cast blame on the other, so they start to doubt their capability.

- **Feeling guilty:** One greatest weapon often utilized by manipulators to absolutely control their victims is to make them feel guilty for nothing. They are constantly put in bad light by their nemesis so that they remain in a dejected or depressed situation. It is quite easy to pull a weak wall down; so also, a mentally weak person can be crushed in no time.

MANIPULATIVE BODY LANGUAGE

It will save you a lot of trouble if you can quickly identify the common manipulative body language used by manipulators. As far as mischievous manipulation is concerned, the main difference between nonverbal communication and verbal communication is that you can spot the troublemaker in the distance before he/she strikes. Nonverbal communication comprises of signs and body language that you can read and interpret, giving you time to strategize and run for cover. On the other hand, verbal communication doesn't give you much time to run for your dear life because once discussing with a manipulator, there is more than 65 percent tendency that he/she may get you.

Familiarize yourself with the following examples of actual manipulative body language adopted by wicked manipulators:

- **Gestures:** Manipulators are fond of using demeaning gestures to control people. They can manipulate people in the way they move their hands, fingers, heads, legs, and arms. Every culture has its different types of gestures that aim to pass across certain instructions, information, or even threats. The manipulators are well aware of the meaning expressed by each gesture. They will concentrate on using those that are meant to threaten people or berate them so that they can make their victims feel uncomfortable and discomfited.

- **Rubbing hands and necks:** When they are trying to get into your psyche and control you, manipulators tend to rub their hands together. This harmless gesture, as well as neck rubbing, is perceived as an attempt to appear nervous and innocent before you so that they can push you into guilt. On most occasions, victims often cave into such gestures in order not to feel bad or evil, without knowing that the manipulators intentionally set a trap for them.

- **Stroking/scratching arm:** Pay attention to people who stroke or scratch their arms when talking with you. Manipulators do that a lot. They are trying to catch your attention, draw you in emotionally, and then control you. It is sad that as harmless this action is, many unsuspecting victims have fallen prey to hypnotists or manipulators.

- **Chin scratching:** It is believed that manipulators can also act like they are clueless when you are discussing with them. When little kids scratch their chins, they are showing their interlocutors that they are momentarily clueless. In an effort to sway your opinions, a manipulator can pretend to be clueless so that you can easily, out of pity, accept his/her sheepish suggestions.

- **Shifting body:** If a person is in an uncomfortable situation, they shift their body positions continuously. When a manipulator wants to make you feel unsettled, he/she will shift his/her body positions several times when you are chatting with him/her.

- **Foot tapping:** People normally tap their feet when they are scared or angry. When a manipulator does so, he/she is trying to dissuade you from taking a firm position about an issue. He/she wants you to jettison your opposition to the matter under discussion.

- **Eye contact:** Normally in communication, people use eye contacts to convey messages nonverbally. However, a manipulator's frown or grimace is an attempt to throw you off balance and take control or charge of the situation. If you are not careful, he/she may turn the situation against you to benefit himself/herself.

DIFFERENT TYPES OF MANIPULATORS

You are likely going to come across different types of manipulators in your life. They don't usually possess the same characteristics and employ similar tactics. That is why it is somehow difficult to quickly identify them. Most of us have spent a great part of our lives cozying up with manipulators, thinking they were our friends, colleagues, or neighbors. Unfortunately, as you would have discovered in this book, manipulators are not after your goodness: They always have some ulterior motives, seeking their own selfish gratifications most of the time.

Could you remember dealing with any of these kinds of manipulators?

- **Covert aggressor:** A covert aggressor has also been called a wolf in sheep clothing. He/she doesn't physically or emotionally present himself/herself as an aggressor or a manipulator. In a critical circumstance, a covert aggressor can even be your mentor, business associate, or your spouse. Take for example, when you are listening attentively to all the pieces of advice your mentor is passing across to you, he/she is busy discrediting your ability to have better achievement. This is why covert aggressors are dangerous. Who else will you listen to other than your mentor? In a similar vein, while you are so passionately sharing your goals and ambitions with your spouse, who is a covert aggressor, he/she is secretly discouraging you from attempting them. A covert aggressor makes you feel inadequate and problematic and causes you to lose your self-esteem.

- **Active aggressors:** We can all immediately spot active aggressors when we meet them. By default, they never try to hide who they really are from people around them. Therefore, active aggressors don't really have many friends or associates because their counter-productive attitudes are not bearable to most people.

- **Passive aggressors:** On the other hand, passive aggressors can be described as the green snakes under the green grass. They don't usually come off manipulative or aggressive, but when given the chance or opportunity, once in a while, they can show their true colors. We all have that friend, uncle, stepbrother, boyfriend or girlfriend who can be unpredictable. Everyone knows that when he/she is pushed to the wall, literally, he/she could be very violent and break or throw things!

- **The ruthless competitor:** The primary reason a manipulator comes into your life is to present himself/herself larger than life over you. He/she shows up to compete with you, ruthlessly. If the need arises, the manipulator could be quite destructive just to make himself/herself at your expense.

- **The heartless criticizer:** Have you ever come across a person who has never seen anything good in others? A heartless criticizer will speak unkindly of everyone. Their evil intention is to make you doubt yourself in everything. You will often see yourself as inexperienced, inadequate, and unworthy of living a better life or achieving something great in your career.

- **The shameless threatener:** It is evident that all manipulators threaten their victims. Beating fear into people's minds is one of the strongest tools or weapons. They threaten to expose you to the public or leak your nude pictures online if you don't do what they have demanded. Before you get into such a difficult position, you must be careful to analyse the behaviors of every new person you meet in your journey in life.

- **The silent treatment giver:** Being given a silent treatment among colleagues or friends could be quite emotionally disturbing or draining. A manipulator can utilize this weapon to undermine your integrity and cause you to be mesmerized. Other people at the place may imitate the silent treatment giver if he/she is in a higher position than you and the rest. You should always remember that what a manipulator wants to achieve is to make you feel less than you truly are.

- **Guilt-makers:** This kind of manipulator makes you feel guilty all the time about things. He/she may be a covert aggressor who is hiding his/her real reason from you but busy projecting all poor attitudes on you. For example, he/she may wrongly accuse you for his/her mistakes because something in him/her convinced him/her that the mistake could have been prevented if you had done your part. Bear in mind that it was his/her mistake, not yours!

RELATIONSHIPS CAN BE MANIPULATIVE

There is somehow a grey area between love and hate in romantic relationships. Many lovers are finding it relatively difficult to differentiate loving relationships from the manipulative ones. However, human senses are designed in a way that we could smell troubles, literally, before they happen. If you are seeing some of the red flags described below, you are probably in or going to be in a manipulative relationship:

- **If you are not really sure if your partner is in love with you or not after dating him/her for several months or years:** Manipulators often do that; they will confuse their partners by keeping them around enough to satisfy their sexual urges or sense of objectification, but not trust them enough to want to marry them.
- **You and your partner always fight instead of sitting down to maturely discuss things.**
- **Your partner often tries to hide many things from you. In other words, he/she is not transparent, and he/she is harboring another agenda.**

- **If your partner is overtly negative:** Knowing that you cannot change anyone, you should be careful starting a relationship with a negative person because they are not going to change their negativity lifestyle overnight.
- **If you often feel that you are being manipulated or controlled by your partner, chances are that you are already in a manipulative relationship.**
- **True love can persevere; however, if your partner often gets angry at the slightest provocation, your relationship is not normal. The same partner would insult you nonstop if you refused to leave the relationship.**
- **When lovers deny each other sex, it is an indication that one of them is manipulative. He/she wants to use "sex" as a weapon to ask for something or make the other person feel unhappy.**
- **No relationship that is marred with resentment can thrive! If your partner is the one that keep malice or remain incommunicado because of a small argument, you are already in a manipulative relationship.**

8

FACING THE FACTS OF HYPNOSIS, BRAINWASHING, AND MIND CONTROL

I n this chapter, you will learn about the three mutually related tools that the dark psychologists often use on their victims or victims-to-be. What you are about to discover will surely shock you! Why? You will soon find out how common dark psychologists utilize these life-wrecking weapons on people.

THE TRUTH ON HYPNOSIS

Let's begin by separating the truth or facts from myths as far as hypnosis is concerned. Highlighted below are the most common myths about hypnosis that people have passed down from one generation to another:

- **Hypnosis will only work on certain people:** It is surprising that some people have held on to this misconception for too long. No wonder they cannot easily detect it when they are being hypnotized. To say the truth, some people may be more susceptible to hypnosis than others, but the truth remains that every human being can fall under hypnosis.

- **Only weak-minded people can be hypnotized:** This is another fallacy that has been widely promoted by those who are truly ignorant about hypnosis. Your mental strength has nothing to do with falling under the influence of hypnosis or not. It can affect all human beings, irrespective of the fact whether they are emotionally strong or weak.

- **Hypnosis is a state of unconsciousness or sleep:** This statement is not absolutely true: When you are being hypnotized, you may feel like you are in a state of sleep, but you are not practically asleep or unconscious. Many victims of hypnosis can still move some parts of their bodies and clearly remember everything they are doing when under the influence of hypnosis.

- **Hypnosis can't be dangerous:** To a certain degree, being put under the hypnotic effect may not be dangerous in itself, but do you know the ulterior motives of the dark psychologist who is putting you through the process? If he/she wants to harm you during that hypnotic moment, he/she has got an upper hand against you because you were in a totally defenseless situation.

That being said, hypnosis is not a completely bad concept because it has been put to a good use in alternative medicine. Have you ever heard of hypnotherapy? It is an alternative medical treatment that utilizes hypnosis to create an ultra-focus condition during which a person may be guided through a series of positive, life-transforming suggestions and imagery meant to impart a better lifestyle or health choice in them.

Some of the medical benefits of hypnotherapy include but are not limited to:

- **Controlling pain:** If you sustain some pain due to burns, childbirth, cancer, headaches, fibromyalgia, joint problems, or dental procedures, hypnotherapy can help you control the pain.
- **Experiencing behavioural change:** Hypnosis has been employed in successfully treating some health problems such as smoking, bed-wetting, overeating, and insomnia.
- **Dealing with hot flashes:** Hypnotherapy can be used to treat hot flashes that are connected with menopause.
- **Treating cancer side effects:** It is possible to treat cancer chemotherapy or radiation effects with hypnotherapy.
- **Managing mental health conditions:** Hypnotherapy has been used to successfully stabilize people with post-traumatic stress, anxiety, and phobias.

How do you know whether hypnosis is being put to a good or dangerous use? The answer to this question may not be as simple as you expect. The rule of thumb is that it depends on who is administering hypnosis on you, and for what purpose? If you are fully aware of the benefits of submitting yourself to the hypnotic procedure, chances are that you are doing it for your own good. Otherwise, a nemesis might be trying to control you for the purpose of robbing you of something that is quite precious to you!

UNDER THE HYPNOTIC STATE

Hypnosis is a system that involves some processes. For you to be truly under the hypnotic state, someone has to perform hypnosis on you. This is contrary to the erroneous belief that we naturally get hypnotized by things that seriously catch our attention, such as a very beautiful and gorgeous lady or a fanciful car or mansion.

A hypnotist utilizes some techniques—known as hypnotic induction techniques—to get you hypnotized. Some of these hypnotic procedures are discussed below:

- **Visualization technique:** During guided visualization, a hypnotist deliberately takes your mind away from things or substances around and ask you to focus on some other things that usually give you joy or good feelings. The hypnotist will also encourage you to concentrate on some beautiful situations that you have experienced before and make you fantasize about enjoying the same great conditions now. For example, if you are the type who enjoy visiting exotic places across the world, the hypnotist can ask you to fully imagine you are in your best place right now while enjoying nature and other nice things the environment has got to offer. You will surely lose yourself in such an eerie feeling.

- **Eye fixation technique:** As its name implies, a hypnotist will instruct you to fixate on a particular object. Sometimes the chosen object will have either spiritual or cultural relevance so that you are enthralled focusing your eyes on it. After some time, your eyes are likely going to get tired of staring at the object. At that moment, you will reflexively close your eyes; you may even fall asleep since the muscles around your eyes have been weakened by the concentrating stare.

- **Rapid induction technique:** This technique is a little dramatic in the sense that it involves the hypnotist dragging you from one place to another, maybe by holding your two hands and pulling you around, shouting "sleep, sleep!". Sometimes, an experienced hypnotist may adopt what is referred to as Eriksson's handshake to pull you around. It is reported that most subjects, who are already shocked by this technique, often resist falling under the hypnotic state. They probably have been scared by the amount of pressure exerted on them by the hypnotist.

- **Pace and lead technique:** What is special about this method is that the subject—you—will act out what the hypnotist is doing or saying. Take for instance, if the hypnotist says that you are in a trance now, you will feel yourself collapsing under his/her hypnosis. In essence, you are strictly following whatever the hypnotist is doing or uttering at that very moment.

- **Physical posture technique:** This technique entails putting the subject in a position that is the most comfortable for him/her to relax. For example, you may be asked to lie down or recline in a sitting position. The best position is the one that can quickly get you to sleep. Falling under hypnosis is expected to bring some flush of relaxation that you don't normally have. All your nerves will be calmed, and your muscles will be soothed.

- **Mirroring technique:** A hypnotist can use your natural inclination to unconsciously copy/imitate what someone else is doing without necessarily knowing that. Have you ever been to the cinema and you unconsciously find yourself acting out (or imitating) what the main actor or your most favorite actor is doing in the film? Hypnosis can work that way, too: All the hypnotist needs to do is to bring up some activities that you love and might likely try to unconsciously imitate. Using that tool, it may be possible for you to be pushed into a trance-like situation in no time.

- **Sensory overload technique:** This method is unique in the sense that the hypnotist is trying to overload your senses so that you are totally blanked out. A hypnotist can overwhelm you with a lot of information, sound, or ideas at the same time to the extent that your mind feels overloaded and disconnected. At this junction, you are no longer assimilating anything, just existing with a blank mind. You will have fallen under the hypnosis when that happens.

- **Stealth technique:** A hypnotist will start to soliloquize with interesting expressions that can immediately catch your attention. Once you are carried away by the sweetness of the hypnotist's monologue, daydreaming about what he/she is saying, your mind can become vapid and weak in no time. In that case, you are already being transported into a faraway land where the things the hypnotist is saying are currently happening!

You may want to ask: Won't I be able to detect immediately that the person I am dealing with is a hypnotist considering how obvious the techniques elaborated above are? Unfortunately, a professional hypnotist can carry out hypnosis on you without you necessarily discovering what he/she is doing. A typical example of this kind are religious leaders who are fond of using hypnosis. People go to their spiritual leaders for prayers, and in the course of this interaction, their spiritual leaders may conduct hypnosis on them. Instead of being careful about what they are being exposed to, the worshippers will be very happy that their spiritual leaders are holding hands with them or laying hands on their heads!

However, the primary reason you are introduced to different techniques used by hypnotists is to open your eyes to their deeds so that you can protect yourself and your loved ones from their deceptive tactics.

ARE WE ALL SUSCEPTIBLE TO BRAINWASHING?

As important as this question is, it is impossible to offer a convincing answer without first understanding what brainwashing is. According to Encyclopedia.com, brainwashing is defined as;

"the technique or process employed in communist-controlled states such as China to attain either or both of two objectives: (1) to compel an innocent person to admit, in all subjective sincerity, that he has committed serious crimes against the "people" and the state; and (2) coercively to reshape an individual's political views so that he abandons his previous beliefs and becomes an advocate of communism. Both objectives, however dissimilar they may initially appear, are attempts to make an individual accept as true what he previously rejected as false and to view as false what he formerly saw as true."

Europe and Americas also have their fair share of ideological and socio-cultural brainwashing, from promoting Marxism, Leninism to democracy, people have been told to embrace a new set of ideologies they may have found distasteful before.

Over the years, brainwashing has moved from being a political weapon to an educational, cultural, military, or religious tool for the singular purpose of misinforming people to their own detriment. The Soviet Police, the Chinese, and Japanese Armies were all brainwashed at one point in time. The purpose of being brainwashed is to create an atmosphere of homogeneity among a group of people so that they can unanimously pursue the same agenda, no matter how spurious and untrue it is.

The process of brainwashing is very simple: It is a "thought control" approach that aims to change the way a person or a group of people think about something through the application of both internal and external pressure in order to achievement, compliance ,or conformity.

Some of the techniques adopted in brainwashing include but are not limited to:

- **Personal humiliation:** Anyone who refuses to follow the pack and accept whatever ideology the group is embracing is usually subjected to personal humiliation. Other members of the group may taunt him/her simply because he/she is standing his/her ground against falsehood.

- **Total control:** The essence of brainwashing people is to absolutely control them. This is very dangerous because they control their thoughts, imaginations, and even the way they act in public. Anyone who stands out or is different is being picked upon in the society. In this scenario, no one is permitted to express their personal opinions or feelings. Everyone must toe the line of the state or the organization controlling their thoughts, even if it is a falsehood.

- **Creation of uncertainty:** When people are always confused about something or find themselves in a condition of uncertainty, they are likely to be taken in—they can easily be brainwashed. So, the primary responsibility of the organization or government brainwashing the people is to constantly keep all of them in a state of flux. When people are confused, it is practically difficult to separate the truth from lies. And it is not difficult for them to swallow everything they had told without questioning its veracity. Take for instance, President Trump, the former president of the United States, wanted people to believe that all Mexicans are drug peddlers or rapist, which couldn't be true. But he succeeded in creating an atmosphere of fear and distrust among the people.

- **Isolation:** Anyone who doesn't want to play along the group mentality is immediately isolated among the group. The other members are encouraged to shun him/her. They are advised not to have anything to do with the rebel or renegade who refused to jump on the bandwagon. Such a so-called rebel can be isolated for a long period of time until he/she becomes psychologically weak and has no apparent option than to join the group and support their evil agenda.

- **Torture:** In extreme circumstances, a renegade might be recommended for some kinds of torture. This is to beat sense into his/her head and compel him/her to toe the line others are supporting. This technique aims at weakening the target psychologically and mentally. Using force to achieve conformity among ranks and files was rife among the Soviet and Chinese Armies during the WWII. This was done to dissuade any soldier from nurturing their individual thoughts and find a cause to oppose the war they had no reason joining in the first instance.

- **Physical exhausting:** The government or organization brainwashing its people sometimes goes to the extent of subjecting them to a situation of physical exhaustion and debilitation to encourage full loyalty. In brainwashing, it doesn't matter how the people feel, the supreme goal is to make sure people are robbed of their human rights to think for themselves. They are only expected to accept the universality, even though it is never substantiated or explained to them. It is like expecting your pet to do exactly as you desire; in that case, your pet doesn't have an option!

- **Destruction of ego and self-esteem:** To force people to comply with harsh rules, the brainwashing agency will make sure that all its subjects do not have self-esteem or ego. They cannot see themselves as a human being that is capable of thinking creatively and solving many life problems by themselves. The agency turns them into thoughtless beings who have to solely rely on what the agency says to make an opinion.

- **Guilt feeling:** In a situation whereby everyone is brainwashed, anyone who attempts to oppose the general misconceptions will be routinely oppressed and called names until he/she becomes guilty for no reason.

- **Alternating fear and hope:** It is the duty of the brainwashing agency to make sure that its subjects are scared into conforming with the laid-down principles. The agency can accomplish this by alternately beating fear and hope into their minds. For instance, the agency can set up a martial law to punish renegades. However, those who are conforming to the generally accepted ideologies will be praised and rewarded. This will put pressure on anyone who is thinking not to follow the crowd to do evil.

Depending on which environment you find yourself, but it must be stated that anyone can be brainwashed. In fact, most people who are brainwashed do not consider the experience to be awful and destructive; they simply considered it a form of loyalty to their nation or organization that is doing the brainwashing.

However, the following categories of people tend to be more susceptible to brainwashing:

- **Emotionally weak individuals:** Those who are emotionally or mentally weak can easily fall for brainwashing. Their lack of inner strength makes them a really easy target for organizations that brainwash people.
- **Those who lack self-esteem:** Anyone who doesn't believe in himself/herself can become a brainwashing subject. It takes self-confidence and trusting one's guts to stand out in a world that is trying to make everyone act the same way.
- **Those who easily feel guilty:** Since they already have that kind of guilt-ridden nature, their nemesis can capitalize on that to brainwash them. Once such a person is overwhelmed by a feeling of guilt, whatever he/she is told becomes only the truth.
- **Insular people:** Insular people are not flexible; they either accept a thing or not. There is no middle ground when taking a position on matters. So, such a person can easily be won over by someone who brainwashes him/her.
- **Those having an identity issue:** Trying to fit in within

a group or a culture can expose you to some ridiculous experiences. Technically, it can make you be susceptible to brainwashing. There are many people in the world who cannot identify with certain cultures—they are willing to absorb the cultures of wherever they find themselves. That's the easiest way to invite culture police who may want to teach you about their culture, thereby brainwashing you. Everyone has his/her intrinsic culture; it is your responsibility to promote your culture and strongly align with it. You can ward off unwanted culture police whose primary duty is to brainwash about how their cultures are more superior to yours.

HOW MIND CONTROL WORKS

Mind control is the process of controlling the mind of a person or the minds of a group of people. To some degree, mind control and brainwashing can be used interchangeably. Why? Because the procedures employed by a brainwashing organization can also be used by someone who is trying to control another person's mind.

Generally, a dark psychologist can control a person's or victim's mind by carrying out any of the following processes:

- **Creating a new identity for their victim:** A manipulator will brainwash you to jettison your identity so that you can be given a new identity that matches the life he/she wants you to assume. It is like an actor changing his/her role in a film. Let's assume you were a nice guy who is very considerate when dealing with others. However, a manipulator may want you to become harsh and merciless by telling you that "nice people never become a millionaire!".

- **Fatigue:** A mind controller will always push you to exhaustion or fatigue until you do exactly what he/she wants. In this case, to avoid being burnt out by his/her endless trouble, you may be pushed to capitulate to his/her will.

- **Repetition:** One of the greatest tools mind-controlling individual or boss uses is to bore you with repetition. Every day, he/she keeps asking you to do the same thing for him/her. To avoid being driven crazy, you will find yourself doing exactly what he/she requests for.

- **Peer pressure:** To compel you to change your mind about something, you may be subjected to intense social or peer pressure. Not many people can stick to their guns when it comes to facing many people in a community wrongly accusing you for something you have not done.

- **Endless criticism:** When someone is trying to change the way you act or behave, he/she may be attacking you every single day. Everything you do will be criticized by the person trying to control your mind. For example, nagging wives are said to possess the power to change their husbands' attitudes over a certain period.

CRIMES INVOLVED

Hypnosis, brainwashing, and mind control have been used to commit some crime in our world. A pedophile can hypnotize his/her victim, brainwash him/her and then end up controlling his/her mind. With these three "weapons of human destruction", so to say, a psychopath can get and keep his/her victim for a long time.

In politics, people have been pushed into committing some acts of perjury and treason after being brainwashed by some politicians. In business, some unlucky business owners have lost chunks of their wealth due to hypnotists that have entered into their heads and controlled them like babies.

In relationships, many people are in a kind of "prison of love" because they have been brainwashed by their lovers who are holding them ransom.

In religions, people have been brainwashed to the extent that they cannot separate the truth from mere fabrication. In various corners of the world, every year there are bloody clashes among people of different cultures, faiths, and ethnicities because they have been brain-washed to perceive one another as sworn enemies.

In education, small children have been taught to hate people for no reason. Anarchists are rising up here and there from the different parts of the world because they had been brainwashed to disregard constituted authorities.

Everywhere basic safety of lives and properties has become of a serious concern as authorities battle members of neo-Nazi and other redskin organizations.

Now ask yourself: Who is the cruelest? Is it the person who brain-washes, mind controls, or hypnotizes? Different people will have different answers to this important question. Whatever your answer is, remember that these three categories of people could be very dangerous. You should be careful how you expose yourself to them and their antics. Many of the problems we have in this world can be avoided if people learn how to keep themselves safe. A lot of people who find themselves in one problem or the other should blame them-selves for not doing enough to protect themselves.

Dark psychologists are a breed of people who lack moral, human feel-ing, and moral aptitude. Their evil intentions superimpose their thinking faculty, and they are usually consumed by what they are going to gain from misleading, maltreating, and misusing others.

In as much as that they lack moral compass with which they could know that their deeds are harmful and can exterminate someone's life, we should put up the strongest defense against them so that they would be able to enjoy an inch of space around us.

It is sad realizing that many people have lost their dear lives due to the evil actions of manipulators, mind-controllers, hypnotists, and other types of dark psychologists.

You are lucky today because their secret is being leaked to you!

9

TWO SIDES OF NLP

N euro-linguistic programming (NLP) is considered to be a pseudoscientific technique employed in communication, psychotherapy, and personal development. It was developed in 1970s in California, United States, by Richard Bandler and John Grinder.

UNDERSTANDING HOW IT WORKS

This section will explain how NLP works. Fundamentally, Neuro-linguistic programming is actually a technique for altering someone's thoughts and behaviors with the hope of making the person display expected outcomes. In other words, if you want someone to act in a certain way, you can apply NLP on him/her and watch him/her do exactly what you had envisaged.

It must be stated that NLP was initially created to solve some medical problems. It has been used in the treatment of anxiety disorders and phobias; it has also been employed in improving workplace performance and personal development.

The NLP system primarily utilizes behavioural, perceptual, and communication methods to facilitate changing people's thoughts and actions. Incidentally, NLP relies on language processing, but you shouldn't confuse it with Natural Language Processing, which has the same acronym.

Highlighted below are the main assumptions that drive the use or application of NLP in altering people's thoughts and behaviors:

- The core concept of NLP is all about the assumption that people operate by internal "maps" of the world which they have acquired or learnt through their sensory experiences.
- So, NLP is applied on an individual for the purpose of detecting and modifying unconscious limitations or biases existing in a person's map of the world.
- While it is not hypnotherapy, NLP utilizes language programming to consciously bring about positive changes in an individual's thoughts and behavior.
- Everyone is assumed to be demonstrating a bias towards one sensory system described as the Preferred Representational System (PRS).
- What an NLP therapist does is detect your PRS by using some phrases such as "I see your point" (indicating a visual PRS) or "I hear your point" (which signifies an auditory PRS).
- Once your type of PRS has been identified, the next step for

an NLP practitioner is to design his/her therapeutic response around that PRS.

- The entire NLP treatment may involve building rapport with the subjects, gathering appropriate information, and setting practical goals with them

It is important that you understand how NLP works so that you can become aware when you are being secretly put through NLP techniques.

USING NLP FOR MEDICAL PURPOSE

The NLP technique is being used for medical purposes, as shown below. In addition to its therapeutic usefulness, the healthcare has found many other ways to apply NLP in order to improve health delivery to patients. Primarily, NLP technique has been used to cure anxiety and phobia disorders. On an expanded scale, it has been used in improving people's personal and professional performances.

Therefore, NLP has dramatically revolutionized healthcare in the following ways:

- **Speech recognition:** Before NLP was used for speech recognition, physicians usually had to dictate clinical report notes to transcribers. Today, with speech-recognition technologies, which incorporate NLP techniques, it is possible for physicians to smoothly have their notes transcribed without having to go through the stress of dictating it.

- **Better clinical documentation:** The application of NLP has drastically improved clinical documentation in the sense that manual and complex structures of Electronic health records (EHRs) have been eliminated. This is due, in part, to the revolutionary text-to-speech capability and an advanced clinical data storage system, all made possible by the adoption of NLP techniques.

- **Faster clinical decision:** Nowadays, physicians can make quick decisions based on the data they have at their disposal. It is no longer cumbersome to process patients' medical records; with the click of a mouse, thousands of medical reports can be retrieved, processed, and sorted out for making precise treatment and prescription. Several decades ago, this improved feature was not available; hence, hospitals faced long waiting hours that led to poor hospital administration.

It must be stated that NLP has contributed immensely to the treatment of social illnesses such as anxiety and depression. People who are depressed may be asked to embrace the following mind-altering principles so as to regain their health:

- **Assurance:** The NLP therapist will assure you that you are not your behavior and that behaviors can be changed. This premise is meant to bolster your belief that you are not responsible for your "anxiety" or "depression". That it just happens to you in the course of living your life. Already, the

NLP therapist is helping you not to feel guilty for a condition you have no power to ameliorate yourself.

- **Capability:** Following the first assurance, the NLP therapist will remind you that you are naturally equipped with all the necessary resources you need to overcome your anxiety or depression. He/she will take you through stories of how other people like you have been able to overcome their problems because human beings are endowed with unlimited capabilities.

- **Feedback, not failure:** In order to completely remove fear from your mind, your NLP therapist will let you know that whatever happens in the course of the consultation should never be perceived as failure: His/her advice should be considered as feedback that must be worked on or improved upon.

- **Better communication is the key:** The primary goal of your NLP therapist is to convince that all you need to change to have a better life is your method of communication. People are often instructed that the people in the world mostly respond to what they heard. And to have a better relationship with people around you, you need to improve your communication strategies.

The good news is that NLP has been successfully applied in helping many people achieve a better lifestyle that is reflected in everything else they do. There are instances whereby someone who used to be a socially reclusive person modify his/her communication strategy and end up becoming an orator or famous presenter on TV.

Despite the fact that Neuro-linguistic programming has been solely used for positive purposes, there are indications that some dark psychologists have also added the technique to their arsenals, applying it on their unfortunate victims.

Having deep understanding of NLP procedures should make you to be wary of being put through these same steps. Your knowledge of NLP system will enable you to free yourself and your loved ones from any manipulator who wants to control your life.

THE OTHER SIDE OF NLP

This is the scariest part: Can the NLP system be hijacked by a manipulator and be used to control the mind of his/her victim? Definitely! In this section, you will unearth some sensitive information about dark psychologists adopting the NLP techniques to manipulate and coerce his/her victims.

The Other Side of NLP entails that a manipulator, armed with the knowledge of how NLP techniques work, can control the mind of another person through:

- **Indoctrination:** Passing negative information into his/her victims' subconscious so that he/she could beat fear into them every day. Speaking words that undermine victims' integrity, self-esteem, and hope is meant to hold them back and prevent them from leading normal lives.
- **Disempowering:** Unlike NLP therapist who tries to empower his/her client, a manipulator's primary goal is to

disempower his/her victims. Why? A manipulator knows that when he/she empowers his/her victims, they would become mentally strong and eventually resist whatever manipulation tactics deployed against them.

- **Lack of education:** When victims of manipulations remain in the dark for so long about the causes of their misfortunes, their manipulators are happy because lack of education will continue to keep them in bondage. Therefore, manipulators will do everything within their power to prevent their victims from getting the necessary education that may turn out to be an eye-opener.

Reading this book is a form of education that a manipulator may want to prevent you from doing. If your friend, colleague, or spouse is responsible for your misfortune, you should be wary when training yourself about how manipulators act. In their evil minds, manipulators believe that if your eyes are open, they won't be able to hold onto you for a long time. In reality, you must seriously guard your heart when interacting with a dark psychologist. If you are not conquered in your mind, you still have a chance to hold your head up.

NLP TECHNIQUES

There are different techniques embedded in the Neuro-linguistic programming system. You and your loved ones will be in a safer place if you could familiarize yourself with the following major NLP features:

1. **Anchoring:** This is the practice of responding differently to a triggering situation. This is somehow similar to classical conditioning. The underlying principle for this technique is that if you keep responding to external stimuli in the same way as you have been doing for years, you are likely going to obtain the same results. For example, if a wife often dismisses her husband's instructions with levity. However, if the same wife turns around and expects her husband to take her words seriously, she may be disappointed because her husband may also choose to treat her shabbily. The only turnaround in their relationship is feasible if the wife changes the way she responds to her husband's words. If she starts showing him some respect and valuing his suggestions, her husband will also change his mind towards her, and they can both enjoy a better romantic relationship. Anchoring, as an NLT technique, provides a unique opportunity to refreshen relationships and helps people to become better at communicating. Imagine a manager that no one loves within an organization because of the way he/she harshly speaks to his/her subordinates. If the same manager decides to be nice and accommodating, he/she will be able to change the unfriendly situations around him/her.

2. **Reframing:** This refers to the practice of identifying adaptive behaviors that can be used in place of some maladaptive behaviors so as to continue to achieve the goals being pursued. In other words, if a student who has been flunking his/her examinations and wants to perform better, he/she can identify the maladaptive behaviors in him/her.

These maladaptive behaviors may include laziness, playing truancy, and not showing interest in his/her studies. The adaptative behaviors to replace the listed maladaptive behaviors include studying harder, attending classes regularly, and learning attentively. When the said student makes the necessary changes in his/her behaviors, better results will be achieved as he/she will be able to pass his/her examinations. NLP is designed to help people improve their rate of performance by consciously taking decisions that could turn things around for good in their lives.

3. **Belief change:** This is one of the primary features of NLP. Everyone is believed to have internalized certain belief system owing to what they are exposed to. Take for instance, we learn from what we see, hear, touch, taste, and smell. Our sensory experiences contribute the largest amount of information that we now internalize as habits. In order to succeed, we must be willing to change our belief systems. A good example to illustrate this issue is that children never harbor any hatred towards anyone; but as they grow up, they start picking hate from what they hear or see from the adults around them. When they grow up, they have already created their own perspective about hatred. To remove this belief system, a new attitude or habit is required. The Behavioural Science claims that it takes people an average of 21 days to create a new habit. To be honest, that isn't a long time. A person with a bad attitude has a lot to lose in life. So, spending time to turn over a new leaf shouldn't be seen as time-wasting.

4. **Future Pacing:** Undergoing an NLP therapy is expected to be a lifelong experience. In other words, an NLP therapist hopes that his/her clients will continue to work on himself/herself so as to achieve success in the long run. Future pacing refers to the practice of continually incorporating good qualities into one's lifestyle for the purpose of remaining mentally and psychologically balanced. It may be hard for someone to keep doing the right things when no one is watching. This is why people attend an NLP therapy with friends and associates so that they can be help one another stay strong and committed.

There is no doubt that NLP was created for a positive and life-enriching purpose. It has become one of the most popular medical features people adopt to change their lives for good. At the same time, some mischievous dark psychologists have been utilizing NLP to constantly harass and mind-control their victims.

How would you know when NLP techniques are being used to destroy you? Well, here are five things you should always look for when undergoing an NLP procedure:

- **Positive energy:** The positive energy that emanates from confidence-boosting words of the NLP therapist are meant to strengthen you psychologically and mentally. Most people with broken spirits cannot easily see or appreciate the good things about themselves. So, soothing and powerful utterances of an NLP practitioner is meant to uplift their souls. If you, by accident, find yourself in an NLP session where negative, morale-destructing expressions are used, be rest assured that you are in the wrong place.

- **It is all about your well-being:** The main reason people go through the NLP processes is to make themselves better, to be more productive, and have more clarity about life. When you see an NLP therapist focusing on himself/herself during an NLP routine, that should be a red flag that you are dealing with the wrong person. Manipulators will always put their own interests ahead of others. In this way, they will violate all NLP rules and leave you worse than you have been before coming to the NLP session.

- **No coercion:** None of the standard NLP techniques require the application of external force or pressure. In other words, there is no coercion when you are undergoing an NLP procedure. If someone who claims to be an NLP therapist is compelling you to do what you think is inappropriate, it is advisable that you should stop such an NLP practice and run for your life. People can only truly change when they are convinced that what they are doing is worth it. Forcing an individual to memorize, internalize, or undertake some processes forcefully will run counter to the underlying principles of NLP.

- **Trust is important:** Those who have successfully gone through the NLP process claim that trust is an integral aspect of the entire procedure. An NLP therapist will first of all try to win your trust by being so nice and understanding with you. You will then, in return, entrust him/her with your time and full participation in the process. Flee from any NLP therapist who is trying to gain your trust through threat, force, or being disrespectful. Normally, you cannot follow the directions or advice given by an NLP therapist whom you do not trust. In short, trust is the building block required to connect wholeheartedly with a therapist and make a success of the entire process.

- **It is your life!** Remember it is your life! If you sense any danger in an NLP therapist, you have the right to bring the whole thing to an abrupt end. We are living in a world where evil people are everywhere masquerading as good people. You can find manipulators everywhere; and they are never ashamed to strike any time. So, use all you have learned from this chapter to protect yourself and your loved ones. It is your life, and it doesn't have a duplicate.

Take it upon yourself to share your discoveries in this book with your friends, colleagues, and relatives who might benefit from them. This is a rare book that exposes all the secret machinations of the dark psychologists so that you can be always seek protection from their evil deeds.

III

PROTECTING YOURSELF

10

ARE YOU A VICTIM?

Now that you are well aware of the dangers dark psychologists can pose to your dear life, it is time for some self-reckoning. Are you a victim of manipulation? To perfectly answer this question, you have to be absolutely honest with yourself. Have you been living in self-denial that you are not a victim of manipulation, hypnotism, or evil Neurolinguistic Programming (NLP)? Or is it possible that you have been a victim of malicious dark psychology without necessarily recognizing it?

The Psychology Today reportedly stated that nearly 2.5 percent of women and 1.3 percent of men in United States who are in manipulative relationships face severe health, mental, and psychological issues. These statistics paint a serious social problem that is begging for immediate solutions.

- Does someone make you feel like you are worthless?
- Do you give more room to someone in your head that you can't get space to accommodate other more important things in your life?
- Are you living in dread of being socially isolated and always craving for attention?
- In fact, has your life been made miserable because someone you trusted took advantage of you and you are so upset about this situation?

If your answers to the questions above are in the affirmative (Yes! Yes!! Yes!!!), then you have been a victim of evil manipulation for some time without realizing it. This is not the time for self-pity; it is time to take some proactive actions in protecting yourself and your loved ones, preventing the same cycle of misery from repeating itself in your life.

PREVENT YOURSELF FROM BECOMING A VICTIM

It is in your power to prevent yourself from becoming a victim of manipulation in the first place. It is assumed that this book has taught you a lot about how manipulators, hypnotists, and other dark psychologists operate. Empowering yourself with this amount of useful knowledge will surely save your life.

How do I stave off a mischievous manipulator? You may want to know. The answers to this important question is not far-fetched.

- **First, learn to say** "No!" Unfortunately, most victims of severe manipulations are kind-hearted and considerate individuals who always say "Yes!" to things or people. We are talking of people who will never do anything to hurt others or put them in harmful circumstances. If you are too kind, manipulators perceive your benign attitude as a weakness. So, they will lunge at you swinging all their destructive shots, because they have realized that you will never say "No" to any of their evil machinations. No one is pushing you to say "No" to everything; you should apply your discretion in selecting what to say "Yes or No" to. The rule of thumb is that you should always say "No" to anything that won't benefit you now or in the future. Take for instance, if a demanding or manipulative lover asks you to follow him/her to Las Vegas to play poker or gamble. And you know down in your mind that you don't know how to gamble. It is totally wrong to sheepishly accept such an invitation and tag along with him/her to Las Vegas. You may end not only losing your hard-earned money, but also losing your precious life.

- **Second, put yourself in a safe position.** More often than not, we are the one opening our doors to manipulators or taking some actions that could draw them to us. Ten years ago, one of my best friends and I won big in the lottery. We shared the money equally because we contributed an equal amount of money to buy the winning tickets. While I deposited my money in the bank thinking seriously about what investments to make or which business to start, my careless friend went on a spending spree. It didn't take long for people around him to know that he had suddenly found some fortune. My friend bought a Rolls Royce, moved into one of the expensive flats in London, which was tastefully furnished. He spent most of his night partying and womanizing. Less than a year later, he started to complain about not having enough money to pay his bills. The rumor had it that one of his many pretty girlfriends used some kind of charm on him and stole a huge chunk of his wealth. On the other hand, I wisely invested mine, and I am still benefiting from the clever decisions I made till today. Never put yourself in a situation that will make you vulnerable to a manipulator's gimmicks.

- **Third, stop being an attention-seeker.** To be honest, manipulators are always searching for attention-seekers. Why? Because it is easy to manipulate them emotionally! When someone's emotions have been used against him/her, such a person is already in a weaker

position or state; he/she will just obediently follow the manipulator's orders. In life, some things are stranger than fiction. We have seen a very strong and confident man turning into a weakling in the hands of a manipulative lady. In the same vein, a woman that is constantly abused finds it very difficult to get herself out of such an abusive relationship. These two unique examples reveal how one's emotion can be used as a trap that is difficult to escape from. It is a common saying that anyone who loves money too much can be magnetized by it. Do you know how many people across the globe have been lured into committing crimes or engaging in prostitution in the name of money?

- **Fourth, validate yourself.** If you are the type who constantly looks outward for validation or acceptance, you are simply putting yourself up for manipulation. Your manipulator already knows that you will surely come for his/her approval before you set out to do anything. That realization, in itself, is scary, because your manipulator can make your life miserable by simply refusing to validate or approve any of your plans. It is not uncommon for friends to seek opinions from one another about which merchandize to purchase, which boyfriend/girlfriend to marry, or which car or house to buy. While it is not a bad thing to do so; your final decision about some important things in your life should come from you. Did you know if your bosom friend was not being truthful about the pieces of advice he/she was giving you? Maybe he/she was speaking out of jealousy or envy. We have seen instances whereby someone's best man or best lady turns around and snatches his/her best friend's husband/wife.
- **Fifth, know what it is in it for you.** Armed with all the essential knowledge about how to easily identify who a manipulator or hypnotist is, you can quickly elude being trapped by their manipulative tricks. If you are dealing with an arrogant, self-centered person, whether a colleague, business associate, or even a relative, that red flag should

warn you to immediately flee for your dear life. Here are
some examples of manipulators you should avoid at all cost:
A business partner who is always speaking for his/her own
gains does not think you stand to gain anything from the
business transaction; a spouse who often accuses you
wrongly and fails to appreciate your sundry contributions to
the relationship. In those people's eyes you do not amount to
anything. They can choose to objectify you and treat you
with all manners of disrespect. So, you should always ask
yourself when in such circumstances: What is in this for me?
If you can't find any cogent reasons for staying in a
relationship or having a business relationship with a partner,
get yourself out of it.

- **Sixth, never blame yourself.** One of the evil intentions
  of a manipulator is to project bad attitudes on you so that
  you can feel sorry for yourself. Take for instance, a
  manipulative boss may choose to always blame you for every
  mistake that occurs at your workplace, even when the said
  mistake was committed by another employee. If you let evil
  people's projections get to you, you will end up blaming
  yourself for an offence you have not committed. So, never
  blame yourself. Stand your ground and defend your cause. By
  doing this, you are inadvertently strengthening your mind
  and putting the manipulator's camp in disarray.

- **Seventh, just disconnect.** Finally, the most sensible
  thing you can do to protect yourself against a manipulator or
  hypnotist is to just disconnect. It is not practically reasonable

to assume that you can outmaneuver a manipulator. Some victims of manipulation who could have saved themselves the embarrassment from the experience and run for their lives chose to stupidly stay in the deceit and harassment. You would have heard some abused women saying: "I will stay in the relationship. I hope I can change him, or he will change". To be honest, no one can change someone who doesn't see anything bad in what he/she is doing. The most honorable step to take when abused, manipulated, or hypnotized is to disconnect yourself from such a horrible experience.

MOST COMMON TRAITS OF A VICTIM

You are halfway to protecting yourself and your loved ones if you have taken some or all of the steps highlighted above. However, the best thing to do is never to invite a manipulator into your life at all. How can you achieve this? In this section, you will discover some common traits that manipulators and users of dark psychology often go for.

Check out below the list and descriptions of common traits that can attract a manipulator to you:

- **Being overtly emotional:** Emotional people are the weakest category of victims manipulators are constantly searching for. All a manipulator needs to do is to tap into their emotion and use it against them. When I was young, there was a kind lady, a Christian down the street who was always willing to help people. Sometimes, she went as far as sharing her meals with those who had nothing to eat, even when it was apparent that the food was not enough for her. Can you believe that she became the main target of many manipulators? Some came to her, begged her to lend them some money only to disappear and never repay their debts. The worst scenario occurred when a man she made friends with reportedly borrowed her car for an occasion. The rumor had it that the manipulator drove the fairly new car across the border into France and never came back.

- **Being Emphatic:** If you are someone who likes to be emphatic about issues, not letting go when you should have, chances are that you may be an easy target for manipulators. When something isn't working in your favor, or when you don't see any reason to stick to it, the best thing to do is to disconnect yourself. Unfortunately, emphatic people are not like that; they want to stay in the game until the end. Many of them, surprisingly, get manipulated in the course of the events. Some people have boyfriends/girlfriends who cannot cook, clean, or even help them when they are in trouble. But because the sex is good, they choose to stay in such a relationship for the long haul until their manipulative lover uses "sex" as a weapon against them.

- **Hypersensitivity:** The primary reason manipulators like hypersensitive people is that they will never let go or disconnect for the fear of hurting others' feelings. An abused wife would like to remain in her marriage because it shameful, in some cultures, to be a single mother. A businessperson who has been defrauded by one of his/her employees may decide not to fire the employee because other workers might be affected by their decision. Therefore, being hypersensitive puts you at the mercy of your manipulator, despite the fact that you have an option to flee or end such an ungratifying relationship.

- **Being lonely/afraid to be alone:** Lonely men and women are mostly susceptible to manipulators' tricks. A manipulator can come into a lonely person's life by first offering some fake companionship. Once you allow him/her to get his/her foot in, the rest will be history. So, even though you are lonely, don't show to the world that you are obviously afraid to be alone. That might cause a manipulator to take an advantage of you.

- **Emotionally/personality dependent**: People who are emotionally/personality dependent on others find themselves easily manipulated by dark psychologists. One of the reasons politicians are popular is that their followers see them as a personality that is larger than life and are attracted to them. Therefore, this makes them worship their political idols like a small god and get manipulated.

- **Afraid to disappoint others**: Not everyone has a stony heart; some people are so kind, sensitive, and considerate that they can inconvenience themselves in order to make others happy. Such a person easily becomes a target for manipulators who knew quite well that the targeted victim is a "Yes, Sir", "Yes, Ma" person. It is a good thing to show consideration for others; however, it is equally harmful to let the whole world think that you are a weakling when it comes to controlling your exuberant emotion.

SIGNS

Manipulators are so crafty to the extent that their victims may not even realize that they are being manipulated. In extreme circumstances, the victims could even pick a quarrel with you for saying harsh about their manipulators whom they have considered to be their benefactors. Recently, a 23-year-old lady shocked the local TV viewers when she said her kidnapper has been good to her and accused the police of interfering with her private life. The report revealed that she was bamboozled by the marathon sex she was getting from the man.

If you are not sure whether you have been subjected to some forms of manipulations or not, the following **seven signs** would help you determine that:

- **Picking holes in all your arguments:** At home, in the office, or among friends, a manipulator will often let you state your opinions first before picking holes or mistakes in them. You see, these kind of manipulators do not appear to be domineering or controlling at first, however, they want you to always feel inferior or incapable in every setting. We all have people like that in our life: It could be an arrogant boss who often likes to belittle his/her employees. It could also be a grandparent or neighbor who never sees anything good in what you do.

- **Manipulation of facts:** A manipulator commonly tampers with facts so as to put you in a disadvantaged position. They hotly debate everything with you and makes you feel uncomfortable whenever you are around him/her. I used to have a teacher like that when I was in secondary. His eyes were always on me in the class, and all answers I gave to his questions were never properly stated. His impudent actions often made me shirk his classes.

- **Those who make you display negative emotions:** In a gathering or at work, a manipulator will always paint you in a bad light. He/she will utter things or take actions that will get on your nerves. The manipulator's primary goal is to push you into a frenzy and cause you to lose your cool. In most cases, the manipulator wants to see you curse, throw punches, and destabilize a meeting. When you demonstrate all those negative attributes, the manipulator has pretty much accomplished his/her mission.

- **Giving you no time to decide:** This sign is common among family members where either of the parents is dictatorial in his/her approach to their children. This can also be found in a workplace where the boss is aggressive and absolutely inconsiderate. Cruel manipulators are really a bother; they do not care whether you have an opinion or not. All they want is that you do exactly what they say.

- **Incessant silent treatment:** Pay attention to this very important sign manipulators use—the incessant silent treatment. No matter what you do to get in touch with a manipulator, he/she will not respond at all to your calls, emails, letters, or otherwise. The singular reason behind this action is to discomfort you or put you in a state of perpetual flustering. Can you imagine someone who claims to be your best friend suddenly going incommunicado with you? Such an experience can lead to emotional depression or anxiety. That is exactly what a manipulator wants to achieve by becoming eerily silent on you.

- **Reverse victimization:** Instead of acknowledging that he/she has made you his/her victim, a shrewd manipulator would act as if he/she is your victim. We could all relate to that! We used to have a neighbor who was rude and self-centered. He would play loud music all day; his dogs would bark from morning to the evening. However, instead of accepting the fact that he was the nuisance, he often accused my family of being too loud and inconsiderate. Why? Because we often welcomed visitors on the weekends, and he alleged that our visitors' cars and deep-throated laughter greatly unsettled him. He had forgot that he was the one making us uncomfortable with the noises emanating from his quarters seven days a week.

- **Transferring the guilt to you:** A few years ago, one man told me a story that made my eyes well with tears. He said one of his employees, who happened to be his sales manager, absconded with a huge sum of stolen money. He had trusted the employee to the point that he allowed him to go to the bank on his behalf to withdraw any amount of money. On this fateful day, the employee cashed out £50,000, but instead of bringing it to the office and handing it over to his boss, he went away with it. When the case was brought to the court, his defense lawyer pleaded with the judge that his client (the shameless thief) was a kleptomaniac right from his childhood. And any huge amount of money could make him misbehave. The guilt was transferred to the boss for not identifying this quality in his employee. Therefore, based on his mental health claim, the employee was ordered to return the remaining amount in his pocket, which was just £10,000. He was eventually set free!

Keep those seven signs in your mind. Any time you detected any of them in someone, immediately take flight. You can also use the same knowledge to save someone else, may be your loved ones.

ACCEPTANCE

Acceptance is an important step that victims of manipulations should take. When you accept yourself the way you are, you would not need any external validation to live a happy life. Many people who look up to others to approve of every plan they make for themselves are inadvertently making them susceptible to manipulation. Dark psychologists often seek out such people.

Even though self-acceptance is hard to achieve, it is something everyone can do. It may take you some time to do it right, but it is definitely worth it. Here are ten practical ways you can increase your self-acceptance:

- Celebrate your uniqueness because you don't need anyone to make you feel awesome about who you really are.

- Let go of things you cannot control. Don't give yourself sleepless nights on what are not essential for your day-to-day survival.

- Identify your strengths and use them to your advantage every time.

- Set some achievable goals and go all out to get them. You will feel more accomplished once you have achieved them.

- Throw a celebration for any accomplishments made, whether small or big.

- Cultivate the habit of planning everything ahead to avoid unexpected disappointments.

- Think positively of yourself and everything that concerns you. It is your business worrying over whatever opinions others have about you.

- Constantly practice self-appreciation by being kind to yourself. Don't be your own worst critic.

- Be actively living. Passiveness will cast a shadow of doubt on your personal capability.

- Seek help from the most reliable people and always remember not to completely let down your guard until you have realized that the person who is mentoring you is not a manipulator.

NEVER BLAME YOURSELF

Whatever situation you find yourself, or whichever uncomfortable experiences the manipulator pushes you through, Never Ever Blame Yourself. Self-blaming is a potent weapon the dark psychologists usually use to rob their victims of their resilient spirits.

Self-blaming will do more danger than you could ever think of. It will make you powerless and weak to confront the manipulators and hypnotists. You will constantly be at their mercies; in that situation, they can get away with whatever they do!

Blaming yourself can, as a matter of fact, increase your anxiety level. You are going to be huffing and puffing about something that was not your mistake in the first instance. Please save yourself of all those negative emotions and live your life happily.

Write it clearly on paper and hang it where you can always see and read it: "I WILL NEVER BLAME MYSELF FOR ANYTHING IN LIFE!" Internalize it, live it, practice it, and preach it. Let it become an integral part of your daily living. Doing this will consequently increase your morale and your mental health will be solid and unyielding to manipulative pressures.

TREATMENT AND THERAPY

Overt or uncontrolled exposure to manipulations could result in a shift in the victim's mental health. After a while, they become violent, erratic, and depressed.

Physicians and therapists do not have a single treatment for people who have been manipulated for a very long time, who are obviously displaying the symptoms of excessive exposure to manipulation. However, they offer treatment for each symptom that is detected in the victim. The essence of the treatment is to help boost the victims' mental health so that they could be mentally strong again.

The list below shows a regimen of medical treatments and therapies used to treat victims of dark psychologists:

～

Symptom displayed by the victim of manipulation

Depression

Possible treatment

Medications and therapies for depression

～

Symptom displayed by the victim of manipulation

Severe anxiety

Possible treatment

Medications and therapies for severe anxiety

～

Symptom displayed by the victim of manipulation

Negative habits copied from the manipulators

Possible treatment

Behavioural therapies

∼

Symptom displayed by the victim of manipulation

Being too negative

Possible treatment

Exposure to positivism and some behavioural therapies

11

SEE IT FOR WHAT IT REALLY IS

"I think it's always important to be vigilant of what you're doing and aware of your surroundings."

— LEONA LEWIS

LISTEN AND OBSERVE

Most of the battles we fight in this life are done individually. In other words, we are solely responsible for own our safety and successes based on the series of actions we take. No one is going to be out there helping you to check out who is trying to manipulate you or not; it is your duty to listen and observe everything in your vicinity. You have to consciously analyse the behaviors of people around you in order to detect any verbal and non-verbal cues that may point out a manipulator or hypnotist.

A DEEPER UNDERSTANDING OF INFLUENCE

You need to have a deeper understanding of how manipulators influence their victims. If you are armed with this knowledge, chances are that you will not easily fall victim to a manipulator's guiles.

One of the definitions of the word "influence" that I really like to use in this book can be found in Merriam-Webster Dictionary. It states that "influence" is "**the act or power of producing an effect without apparent exertion of force or direct exercise of command.**" As harmless as their physical actions may seem, the primary aim of a manipulator is to make their victims' lives miserable.

How do they necessarily accomplish this? The influence dark psychologists exert on their victims come in different forms, some of which are described below:

- **Neutral influence:** As cunning as many dark psychologists are, they will pretend that they are not directly connected with your misery, meanwhile they are mainly responsible for the untold hardships you are going through. A manipulator can delegate another person, maybe your close associate or even your spouse, to directly influence every decision you make. If you are not quite suspicious, you may be fighting the wrong person while your main nemesis is hiding in the shadow. In certain cases, you may even end up going to your manipulator to seek advice about what you should do about your situation, not knowing he/she is the one calling the shots.

- **Positive influence:** As its name implies, everyone desires to be positively influenced, in as much as we believe it is for our good in the long run. But you should be careful about this; manipulators don't necessarily first appear in front of us as manipulators—they can begin as your mentor, leader, boss, or even your lover. To a certain degree, they will try to influence us positively by offering pieces of advice meant to grow us personally and professionally. They will show us love and cares; they will handle our case with all dedication and selflessness. Who doesn't like to be affectionately spoiled? However, by the time they have entered into our heads and won our trust, they would strike, showing their real nature.

- **Negative influence:** Those who are following the wrong crowd may receive some negative influence from their group or gang leaders and members. A saying goes thus: "You are who you associate with". Ten years ago, one of my friends, Fred, had had a sudden transformation that obviously shocked his parents and friends alike. Fred was such a quiet bloke, always shy and self-effacing. During his work experience at a local bank, he met a guy who introduced him to drinking and womanizing. Fred captured his colleague's habits in no time and became so bold that he could walk up to any lady and woo her. And when he drank beer, he wouldn't stop until dozens of beer bottles littered his bedroom. That was how far negative influence could ruin a person's career and life!

- **Life-changing influence:** Some influence on people could be life-changing, for better or for worse. If anyone is coming to you demonstrating some attitude of selfishness, please wake up; he/she could be a manipulator. Whatever you do in association with others, in as much as it is not for your own good, think twice before you continue going down that path. We are endowed with a natural instinct with which we could sense some dangers far before they occur. I don't remember who said it, but there is an important lesson in this quote: *"An insincere and evil friend is more to be feared than a wild beast; a wild beast may wound your body, but an evil friend will wound your mind."* Let us always remember that we have the right to reject any unwanted act of influence over our life. If we fail to do so, we may find ourselves being subjected to continuous manipulation that may leave us more damaged than we could ever imagine.

INFLUENCED BY ANOTHER PERSON'S BODY LANGUAGE

Body language (also known as kinesics) is one of the commonly used non-verbal tools in communication. Over the years, people have passed information across from one person to another using different types of body language. At the schools for people with impaired hearing, body language has been utilized in educating a generation of people that might have otherwise been uneducable. As we celebrate the good applications of body language, it is sad to realize that dark psychologists also employ this communication to influence and take advantage of another person.

Highlighted below are the most common types of body language used by manipulators:

TYPES OF BODY LANGUAGE

You have read about some types of manipulative body language in Chapter 7. In this section, you will read about additional kinds of body language that dark psychologists are also using.

- **Squinting or looking slyly:** Squinting is perceived as a seductive gesture if it is done by a man to a woman, or vice versa. As harmless it appears, it can make someone restless and confused if it is done by a total stranger. Most especially, a lady may be thrown off balance if a man she has never met before continues to look at her slyly for hours. This feeling of discomfort may make the target or lady lose focus on whatever she was doing at that time. Manipulators have used this body language successfully to confuse and command their victims' feelings for minutes, hours, or days, depending on how often they can lay their eyes on their victims.
- **Clicking fingers:** A manipulator can click his/her fingers, whether noisily or noiselessly, to draw your attention to himself/herself. It is a ploy or tactic they usually use when they want to unsettle you and make you doubt yourself. Take

for instance, you may be in a meeting where you are offering your opinions on the issue under discussion. Immediately your senior manager, who is chairing the meeting, begins to click his/her fingers, you are likely going to be checking yourself whether what you are saying is reasonable or not. If you have not been aware of the fact that such a gesture could be used to manipulate you, there is every possibility that you may be forced to abruptly conclude whatever you are saying.

- **Nose-Picking:** Even though it is an asocial behavior, some people pick their noses to express some displeasure at whatever they are seeing or hearing. If you don't have enough confident, you may be responding to such a gesture from time to time.

- **Deep-breathing:** When you are interrupted by someone who deep-breathes "Hmm!" several times when you are talking, he/she is trying to give others a negative impression about whatever you are saying. He/she may want other people to doubt the truthfulness of your words.

- **Incessant yawning:** When a person yawns often when you are saying something, he/she is either showing that you are talking too much, or that your words do not make any sense to him/her. Yawning is a sign that he/she is bored with whatever you are saying.

- **Tongue-clicking:** When someone clicks his/her tongue when you are contributing to a discussion, he/she is trying to alert other people that you are lying. Continuously clicking their tongues is a crafty way manipulators undermine the significance of what their victims are saying.

- **Fake coughing:** A manipulator can cough several times to dissuade his/her victim from expressing his/her confidence on an issue. The coughing is fake, and almost everyone understands what it means—it simply indicates that the cougher disregards what the victim is saying or alleging.

As innocuous as the above-mentioned forms of body language are, they have been used repeatedly by manipulators to render their victims weak and powerless in meetings, among other colleagues, and in family get-togethers.

REMAINING NEUTRAL

You may have heard about the different coping strategies people adopt when it comes to dealing with manipulators; one of the most effective strategies is to maintain a neutral baseline behavior without any bias. What this entails is that you should never express extreme emotions about your circumstances.

It is almost impossible for a manipulator to completely take over your senses if you always operate in neutrality. In other words, if a seducer-cum-manipulator comes to you using all his/her tricks to seduce you, if you are the type who responds modestly to seduction, a seductive manipulator will have little or no influence on you. In the same way, if you are not consumed by greed and illogical love of money, it is almost impossible for fraudulent manipulators to get you.

In principle, a neutral behavior is comparable to being neither cold nor hot about any issue. This frame of mind is required to checkmate every move a manipulator makes towards you. **This is how it works**: If you come to me and spend hours telling me how profitable a deal is going to be, how much millions of pounds I am going to make from the business, and how easy it is to execute it. If I do not appear a sceptic to you as well as not expressing excitement about the deal, you are likely going to misjudge my reactions: You may think I don't like doing the business with you. In that scenario, you, the manipulator, will not be interested in wasting your time convincing a doubter.

More often than not, people bring manipulators into their lives by the way they express their emotions when baited. Usually, dark psychologists will throw their prospective victims some baits and watch carefully how they will react to them. If you don't exude overexcitement about their baits, manipulators are likely going to be confused about how to handle you.

Neutral behavior is replicable; in other words, you can develop it if you undertake the following procedures:

- **Live without any bias:** Don't be too quick to assume that something is good or bad for you. Give it time and see if it will eventually be good for you or not. For the fact that one of your relatives introduced a business idea to you doesn't mean he/she couldn't cheat you in the business. If I were you, I would welcome any suggestions from my spouse with a neutral mindset. In that way, when things go wrong, I would not live the rest of my life biting my fingers. Doesn't that action make you a natural sceptic? Not at all! When dealing with a potential manipulator, you should do everything in your power to protect your heart. If a person is not already conquered in his/her mind, such a person still has some hope that he/she would overcome every deceit of the dark psychologists.

- **Never accept anything at face value:** When you cultivate the habit of not accepting things as they are presented, you will see that everything has another side. Most dark psychologists won't let you see their other sides when finding a way to get into you. So, if you have been careful from the outset, you will have made it very difficult for them to pitch their tents with you.

- **Use your mental analyzer:** Quickly analyse with your head if this person seeking your attention and time worth getting it. We all have instincts that will let us know we are playing with trouble by opening our heart or door to a manipulator. If at that instant you feel some uneasiness creeping over you, quickly excuse yourself and cut off the communication. A manipulator won't be so violent at the beginning or else he/she won't have a chance to craftily get into you.

- **Momentarily embrace a second thought:** Most of the victims of manipulation often blamed themselves later for not having a second thought about their manipulators when red flags were all flying everywhere when they first came into contact with them. When unclear about what to do about a sudden proposition from acquittances, relatives, and strangers, please have a second thought about it.

INCREASING YOUR AWARENESS

You are reading this book now because you want to increase your awareness about how to prevent dark psychologists from messing up your dear life. The truth is that the actual process of protecting yourself during the acts of dark psychology can be hard to achieve, and the main method you can adopt is to increase your awareness to prevent it from happening in the first place.

What steps can you take in achieving this? In Chapter 10 you have read about the seven signs that reveal the devious acts of the dark psychologists. Here, you will learn how to counter dark psychologists' tactics without actually causing a stir:

- **Stand your ground:** Whether you are in a meeting or a family get-together and a manipulator is trying to pick holes in your arguments or words, stand your ground! If you confidently support your position or argument with convincing evidence, you are likely going to force the manipulator to keep his/her mouth shut.
- **Call for evidence:** If you find yourself in a dire situation where your detractor, a manipulator, is trying to manipulate facts against you, ask him/her to show his/her evidence. In the absence of any sensible evidence, your tormentor will lose face for making an evil attempt to destroy you.
- **Practice neutral behaviorism:** The most potent way to prevent anyone from rousing negative emotions in you is to practice neutral behaviorism. Don't be unnecessarily attached to anything. Just let things fly and never be afraid to have a

second thought about them. You know what? What makes you angry in one second can become a ridiculous issue that will crack you up in loud laughter the next second.

- **Ask for the rules of engagement:** Don't let anyone put you in a box that you don't belong in. When having a meeting or relationship with someone who turns out to be a manipulator, always ask for the rules of engagement. Why are we doing this, and what are the rules we are playing by? It would be difficult for just one person or a group of people to isolate you, keep you incommunicado, accuse you wrongly, or make you feel guilty when the rules of interaction have already been laid down and each party is expected to play his/her part accordingly.

GOING WITH YOUR INTUITION

There is no hard-and-fast rule when it comes to dealing with dark psychologists, who often come in different forms and categories.

This is why it is imperative you go with your intuition in whatever approach you adopt. You should weigh the pros and cons of going with one's intuition, and in the end, if your gut feeling tells you that something is inappropriate or wrong, it is better to be safe than sorry.

We are built differently, and each of us has his/her unique way of detecting danger that hasn't happened yet. It is a kind of in-built intuitive system developed over one's lifetime. Don't regret later for not paying attention to what your body, so to say, is telling you.

You will never go wrong to do things that will protect you from unkind actions of shameless dark psychologists. More so, pay attention to every revelation made about them in this book and share them with your loved ones so that they too could be fully aware of the danger looming in the dark outside.

12

RAISING YOUR WALLS

"The most common way people give up their power is by thinking they don't have any,"

— ALICE WALKER

YOU HAVE RIGHTS

Let this ring loud and clear in your mind all the time: You Have Rights! Irrespective of where you live or what culture you come from, there are local and national laws enacted to protect your human rights.

Human rights, as defined by Oxford Learners' Dictionary, is **"one of the basic rights that everyone has to be treated fairly and not** *in a cruel way, especially by their government."* A dark psychologist that subjects you to a series of damning actions has violated your fundamental human rights. Hence, he/she is liable to be punished under your local and national laws.

A manipulator has treated you unfairly and cruelly, and he/she should be handed over to the appropriate law enforcement agencies for prosecution. However, when you are dealing with a very clever manipulator, he/she may not leave any traces for you to discover he/she is behind your ordeal. In that scenario, you probably have nothing to use against him/her as evidence.

When dealing with cunning dark psychologists, always make sure you document everything. If the manipulator poses himself/herself as a business partner, you can record every meeting or ask him/her to append his/her signature to every business deal you both agreed on. You will be able to use those pieces of evidence to seek some legal redress.

However, don't get carried away, what most dark psychologists are seeking, is your mind so that they can easily manipulate your emotions. In that case, it is almost impossible to quantify the extent of the damage they have done to you.

The Article 5 of the United Nations Universal Declaration of Human Rights states that *"No one shall be subjected to torture or to cruel, inhuman or degrading treatment or punishment."* In so far that your country is a member of the United Nations, you are protected by this charter. It aims to protect you from mental or emotional assaults meted out by dark psychologists.

When you know your human rights, you will have the confidence to prevent anyone from undermining them.

MANAGING YOUR EMOTIONS

"The sign of an intelligent person is their ability to control their emotions by the application of reason."

— MARYA MANNES

Controlling one's emotions may not be as simple as it appears, but the good news is that everyone can successfully manage their emotions if they try. It is imperative that you learn how to manage your emotions so that you can properly protect yourself.

Highlighted below are some practical approaches anyone can adopt in controlling his/her emotions:

- **Just pause for a little while:** When you discover that your emotions are running wildly, and they are in the process of getting the best of you, please pause for a short time. If you are in a condition whereby negative emotions overwhelm you and you don't necessarily know how to keep your thoughts under control, please stop! One great technique often used to stop a flood of negative thoughts is deep breathing. Refrain from saying anything, just breathe deeply for some minutes. It is helpful if you could decide to change your environment for a short time or leave the presence of the cruel dark psychologist rousing negative thoughts in you. If you could do those suggested actions, you would feel a lot lighter as the negative thoughts begin to disappear from your mind.

- **Positive affirmations or rehearsals:** Psychologists believe people can replace the negative thoughts flocking to their minds with positive affirmations. Take for instance, if you are overwhelmed about the thought of losing your wealth, you may replace that annoying thought with a positive affirmation such as: "**My wealth is everlasting! I will live till old age in great wealth!!**" Repeating this positive affirmation from time to time helps you sound the negative voice that has been keeping you unsettled for some time. Positive affirmations are also referred to as "positive rehearsals". You constantly tell your subconscious or mind great and wonderful things about you, about your current and future circumstances. By doing this like a routine, you are likely able to recreate a positive and powerful mindset that you need to achieve tangible successes in life.

- **Hear but don't speak:** We could call this a biblical mind-conditioning technique. It is written in James 1:19 (King James Version), that "*Wherefore, my beloved brethren, let every man be swift to hear, slow to speak, slow to wrath.*" It doesn't matter whatever your manipulator is saying to irk you, this technique advises you to listen, but refrain from saying anything at all. Hence, if you do just that, you will be able to control your angry reaction and keep the situation under control. Remember that the primary goal of a manipulator is to see you troubled, angry, and unsettled. It is your power to prove them wrong and confuse them in their strategy.

There are other ways people use to control their emotions. However, we are only recommending the positive techniques described above. It is equally important to differentiate the helpful methods from some harmful ways people have been utilizing in managing their emotions.

Let it be clear that the following are not recommended for controlling your emotions: If you adopt any of the harmful approaches described below, you are inadvertently doing more harm to yourself than any good:

- **Use of mind-altering substances or drugs:** You may be able to temporarily control your mind by abusing drugs or other substances, but in the long run, you are doing a serious harm to your body and life.
- **Binge-drinking:** There are some people who often boast of keep "calm" by consuming a lot of beer and alcohol. To be honest, anyone who does so is only putting himself/herself up for some damage in his/her body. Stay away from binge-drinking.
- **Denial:** It is funny for people to control their feelings by living in denial. Unfortunately, reality will soon strike while they are trying to hide their true feelings from what is exactly happening to them.

- **Attachment:** It is common for people to attach themselves to lovers, friends, nice colleagues, and neighbors as they try to overcome some uncomfortable experiences in their lives. Be careful: No one can be trusted, and they make yourself vulnerable through unreasonable attachment to people. If care is not taken, you may be running from Peter only to get pummeled by Paul.

BUILD YOUR SELF-ESTEEM

Your self-esteem is exactly how you feel about yourself. People with low self-esteem often look down on themselves; they usually belittle their own achievements and seem to be suffering from inferiority complex. When your self-esteem is pretty high, it will take a stranger some tough time before he/she can enter into you.

Understand that having a high self-esteem is not the same as being unreasonably arrogant. It means that you know your worth and won't do any senseless thing to put yourself in a risky situation where anyone will take advantage of you. Dark psychologists are always looking for those with low self-esteem so that they can make their lives unbearable for them.

With this information, it is imperative that you build or improve your self-esteem. By doing this, you will avoid turning yourself into a victim.

You can boost your self-esteem by doing some or all of the processes highlighted as follows:

- **Channel your inner superstar:** We all have a superstar in us that is begging to be revealed to the world. Realizing that you are born with some inherent skills, talent, and uniqueness will always equip you with the right amount of confidence that you need to face any situation in this life. Those who look down on themselves and their abilities are possibly in doubt whether they are born with any talent or not. If you can just let your inner superstar speak for itself once in a while, people around you will respect you and hold you in high esteem. One of my university friends was the shyest person I have ever seen in my life; he was so timid to the point that he simply could not look anyone in the eye. One day, we were in an important event and everyone there agreed that he should be the Master of Ceremony. After his initial resistance, he surrendered and mounted the podium. Everyone was already simpering because we knew doing public speaking wasn't his thing. It was like throwing fish into a pot of hot water. After mumbling for a few minutes, he summoned up courage and obviously shocked all of us there with his hidden oratorical gift none of us had ever detected in him. The bottom line: Bring out the hero in you and show it to everyone.

- **Be mindful of everything:** It is dangerous to live thoughtlessly around a dark psychologist. It is like living in a vacuum where one doesn't have a grip on the events happening around him/her. Only hopeless or downtrodden people live thoughtlessly. You should be that person who actively participates in everything occurring around you.

Show the world that you have a strong personality, and that you are not a push-over for any manipulator. When we were in secondary school, it was not the prettiest girl or the most handsome guy that was too difficult to get; it was those loud and difficult ones that often gave guys/girls tough time before agreeing to becoming their friends. Do you know that there is nothing like an old or young politician when it comes to finding supports to pass a new law? Even an MP that had served for decades of years must seek out those newly elected MPs, no matter how young they are, to get their support to move his/her legal agenda forward. This indicates that when you present yourself as a formidable personality, people will have to ask for your permission before getting themselves into your space. In the same way, a manipulator will think twice before approaching someone who is very confident and well aware of the things going on around him/her.

- **Live in the present:** Your past is none of your business, and you should never allow it to shape or define your current lifestyle. One of the evil things people do to themselves is to stick to their inglorious past and let it rob them of living an amazing life. If you were a failure before but your situation has changed for the better, please embrace your present "you" with pride and boldly speak with authority. As long as you are holding onto your uneventful past, you are making yourself unqualified or unfit for a wonderful, new experience. Dark psychologists understand that they can easily use your past to hold you ransom.

- **Don't compare yourself with anyone:** The best way to avoid throwing yourself constantly into a despair is to stop comparing yourself with others. Everyone is unique; we do things differently and our results are not the same. What you are capable of achieving, it may be difficult for others to record similar level of success. Even twins that were born on the same day never grow up acting in the same way—they are genetically and behaviorally different. Albert Einstein once cautioned those comparing themselves with others in one of his popular quotes: *"everybody is genius. But if you judge a fish by its ability to climb a tree, it will live its whole life believing that it is stupid."* Nothing kills a person's esteem faster than comparing himself/herself with others.

- **Take good care of yourself:** Pay attention to your health and stay alert. Exercise and eat good food. Take care of your physical appearance, always present yourself neat and well-dressed. Remember that first impressions matter a lot. More so, you need to have enough sleep and rejuvenate your brain so that it can function properly. When you neglect your self-care, you may end up suffering from stress or other illnesses that may hinder you from presenting a glorious image of you to the world. If a manipulator is thinking of getting into you, but he/she sees that you have a good physique and mental sharpness, he/she will re-think his/her plans. Sometimes, people unintentionally invite dark psychologists to attack them by the way they weakly present their personas. It is just common sense to think that a weak person will become an easy victim. And that is exactly how dark psychologists think!

SAYING "NO"

You can't believe how high a wall of protection you can raise by simply saying "No!" Kind-hearted and considerate people often think that they are making the world a better place by generously saying "Yes!" to everyone. To some degree, they may be right; the world needs kind and caring people who are always willing to offer a helping hand to those in need.

Unfortunately, dark psychologists don't reason the same way. They perceive kind-hearted people as weaklings that they can easily take advantage of. Good people are hurt the most in this wicked world, and that is why you must learn how to say "No".

Train yourself to identify what works for you and what doesn't. Remember that saying "No!" doesn't mean that you are rude or inconsiderate; it just signifies that you are no longer going to put yourself in a situation where you are vulnerable to dark psychologists' assaults and manipulations.

More so, you should never feel guilty for saying "No", even if the other person keeps on insisting on getting a "Yes". You should emphatically say "No" in the following situations:

- When the matter under discussion adds no measurable value to you or your business. You don't want to give room for interactions that will waste your precious time and allow a total stranger to get a foothold in your life.

- If the purpose of the connection violates the human rights of others. It is criminal to undermine the fundamental human rights of others. You may be liable to criminal charges for doing so.
- If it contradicts your personal principles or ideologies. Take for instance, if you are the type of person who dislikes falsehood and underhand business dealings, you should immediately say "No!" when someone is suggesting such things to you.
- When you suspect that you are interacting with a manipular or a dark psychologist.
- If you are not made the center of the conversion, and your interlocutor appears manipulative in words and body language.
- When your gut tells you that you should say "No". Sometimes you may not feel convinced about something. At that moment, your body wants you to say "No" to whatever the other person is suggesting.

There are no fixed rules about what you should say "No" to. At this junction, you should use your discretions and follow your instincts. Not everything that glitters is gold; sometimes what you think is tangible and worth exploring may turn out to be a waste of time for you. In an extreme circumstance, they could be traps that will lure you into the dragnet of a dark psychologist.

BE SKEPTICAL

Never take any information or suggestion at face value or as it is presented; it doesn't matter if it is coming from your spouse, friends, or business partners. You should cultivate the habit of always scrutinizing facts to be sure you are assimilating nothing but the truth. Be so skeptical that everyone around you knows that you are not gullible.

There are times when people get deceived by believing information that cannot be quantified. Some people have complained of being duped and manipulated by palm readers, shamans, or spiritualists who helped reveal some vague information about their future. In essence, this practice is referred to as the 'Barnum Effect'.

Some people have the habits of listening attentively to palm readers or spiritualists who claim to have had the supernatural powers to see far into the future. It is not uncommon to see people visit those kinds of spiritualists every week to hear more prophecies about different aspects of their lives. In turn, the shamans or spiritualists hold a lot of influence on them and, when necessary, manipulate their victims' thoughts and actions.

The spiritualists have, in certain situations, capitalized on the absolute trust their victims reside in them to defraud them, getting money and other properties from them. It is almost impossible how many millions of people worldwide have lost huge chunks of their personal wealth consulting fortune-tellers.

PREVENTING AND BREAKING FREE FROM HYPNOSIS, BRAINWASHING, AND MIND CONTROL

Most of the information presented in this book is about how to prevent yourself from becoming a victim of a dark psychologist and breaking free from Hypnosis, Brainwashing, and Mind Control. There are two main ways you can accomplish this:

- **Understanding who you are:** Do you have a high self-esteem? Are you capable of frustrating every tactic a dark psychologist deploys to catch you? Do you know that, paraphrasing Mahatma Ghandi, *"No one can hurt you without your permission?"* After doing some self-analysis and discovered you are still found wanting in some areas of your life, it is very important that you strengthen those areas before putting yourself in the public. Dark psychologists are always on the lookout for weak-minded people to prey upon.
- **Strategize your defensive mechanisms:** You have learned a lot of defensive mechanisms in this book that can help you avoid the possibility of becoming a victim of hypnotism, brainwash, and mind control. Now, it is time you designed a defensive strategy that will work best for you. This may entail combining a few of what you have already read about in this book. Take for example, you may need to improve your self-esteem, learn how to say "No!" emphatically, master your body language to drive away

potential manipulators, and refrain from being publicly emotional.

DEVELOPING YOUR POKER FACE AND OTHER BODY LANGUAGE

The best weapons to use against an enemy, as they say, are the same ones he/she uses to attack you. This aphorism is true on most occasions. When you are dealing with a manipulator, it is sensible to learn some of the body language and signs he/she is using to oppress you. You will then use them back on him/her.

One of the potent weapons you can develop is a poker face and other related body language. When you wear a poker face, you are intentionally confusing your enemies, because they cannot accurately read your emotions. They cannot confirm whether you are happy, sad, or having mixed emotions. More so, you can also employ some body language which you believe will protect you from a dark psychologist, most especially from people who use body language as a means of manipulation.

Other body language techniques that you can focus on include:

- **Cold reading**: This refers to a practice of obtaining a great deal of information about someone by analyzing his/her behaviors, age, fashion, gender, hairstyle, body language, manner of speech, education, sexual orientation, religion, and so on.
- **Mind reading**: This is about reading a person's mind

without necessarily asking him/her any questions. This practice requires some preternatural power or telepathy, and two individuals can communicate with each other without using their five senses.

- **Lip reading**: When dealing with a manipulator who speaks other languages than the one you understand, you can use lip reading to predict the person's behavior through the way he/she pronounces words.

13

IN A RELATIONSHIP WITH
DIFFICULT PEOPLE

I f you are in a relationship with a difficult person, there is every
possibility that a certain form of manipulation exists in that relationship. In reality, people don't get attracted to anyone they don't
have natural affection for. However, staying in a relationship with
someone you hate indicates that you are either being manipulated
unknowingly, or the other person has stayed in the relationship
because he/she has already objectified you and deriving maximum
pleasure from that.

MANIPULATIVE AND TOXIC RELATIONSHIPS

We have probably seen examples of manipulative and toxic relationships all around us. By default, a toxic relationship is the one in which
those engaged in it are unhappy about such an alliance. Unfortunately,
most of those involved in manipulative and toxic relationships some-

times find it very difficult to call it quits because of something that binds them together.

Some common examples of toxic relationships include:

- **Controlling relationships:** One of the people in a relationship can be so controlling that he/she chooses to treat the other with absolute disrespect. A controlling partner will tell you everything you have to do in the relationship, to the extent of choosing the kinds of clothes or shoes that you should wear every day or what types of food or drinks you are allowed to consume. This kind of attitude will make the other involved in the relationship feel like a powerless person who is being bossed around. When you see someone who is henpecked, he/she is always unhappy with his/her partner. At every slightest misunderstanding, they could end up punching each other in the face. This level of toxicity could result in health issues or even mental health problems.

- **Jealous people:** Everyone has a certain degree of jealousy in them but being in a relationship with a very jealous person could become a serious nightmare. Your phone will be secretly checked; all your private messages will be gone through to detect if you are cheating, even when there are no reasons to embrace such a suspicion. People in a jealous, toxic relationship are often affected by anxiety, because they could never imagine what their jealous partners are up to. Pathological jealousy, which is otherwise known as Othello Syndrome is considered to be very dangerous because the jealous partner could be absolutely delusional and obsessive. In one of the rare studies conducted on delusional jealousy in the United States in 1998, where 20 participants were randomly chosen and 13 of them were men. The research revealed that out the 13 men, 9 actually attacked their spouses. A weapon was used by three of them and 12 had harmed their spouses. This reveals the extent of inconvenience associated with a toxic relationship.

- **A negative thinker:** There is no way a negative thinker can make a beautiful relationship with anyone. Every single thought in his/her heart is evil. Even if you are doing your best to impress him/her, your good gesture will still be misinterpreted. You know, sometimes, people who have had a traumatic experience in the past will always be suspicious of the actions of others, irrespective of how great they are. This is why it is imperative that you spend time to study people very well before falling in love or starting a relationship with them. You may be fortunate to have discovered earlier on that such a person may not be the best fit for you.

- **The nagging one:** This doesn't need a lot of explanation: A nagging wife/husband is a complete pain in the butt. In this kind of relationship, you get talked down to like a baby. All your actions are questioned, and your decisions are weighed thoroughly for the purpose of finding some faults to spend days whining about. It is only in a family that a nagger can make life unbearable for others. If you happen to work with a nagging colleague or boss, you will find the most of your working hours devising ways to handle such an occupational disturbance. Only a few workers can survive in an atmosphere where they are constantly accused of one wrong or the other. Such an action will kill their motivation, and they may be constantly unproductive in that environment.

- **Cheaters:** Whenever cheating enters a relationship, it is like a fire has been thrown into a bush—it will burn everything in its path. The partners will begin to doubt everything they do, accusing each other angrily. Most of the domestic abuse cases in the United Kingdom is attributed to infidelity. This is why it is not surprising that the most commonly cited reason for divorce in the UK is infidelity. According to the Global Investigations statistics, the percentage of married women who admitted to being unfaithful rose 40 percent from 10.5 percent in 1990 to 14.7 percent in 2010. In the same fashion, up to 57 percent of males revealed they had cheated at least once in their relationship. Those who are trapped in a cheating relationship where the partners are accusing each other of infidelity knows that it is not always an easy place to be.

- **The liar:** No good relationship can be established on falsehoods. If you are in a relationship with a liar, you are already putting yourself up for regular abuse and manipulation. It may be difficult for you to identify who a liar is when meeting them for the first time. However, if you can be patient and study them, chances are that you may be able to see them as they are, and not as they portray themselves. One thing about staying in a relationship held together by habitual lying is that you will never get to know the truth about the other person. We have seen it in films how conmen borrowed expensive cars to deceive gullible ladies that they are rich. Once they have swept such ladies off their feet, they will do everything in their power to keep their identities hidden by escalating their lies.

- **Abusive relationship:** In the United Kingdom, the statistics of abusive relationships paint a gloomy picture. It is estimated that 1 out 4 women, and 1 out of 6 men are subjected to some forms of abuse in relationships. The sad reality is that this abuse leads to an average of two women being murdered every week and about 30 men losing their dear lives to abuse every year. Domestic abuse accounts for 16 percent of all violent crime in England and Wales and has more repeat victims than any other crime. One of the headaches associated with abusive relationships is that those involved often pass the blame to the other person. There is a lot of psychological projection going on, with each partner projecting blame on each other. In this case, it will be practically difficult for them to sit down and solve the problem amicably as none of them is accepting the blame for causing the abuse.

- **An insecure partner:** Those who have been in a relationship with an insecure partner often complain that it is totally toxic and manipulative. Instead of embracing the fact that he/she is somehow insecure and do something about it, the person may be acting erratically to present himself/herself as someone he/she isn't. It takes two to tango; unfortunately, if one of them lacks the confidence to tag along, such a relationship may be problematic.

- **A demanding person:** A demanding person is manipulative in nature. He/she doesn't have any considerations for others. All he/she wants is that his/her orders be carried out immediately, and without any questions. Why many relationships turn sour is that when you demand too much from your partner, they are likely going to feel that they are being used. In a relationship where one partner objectifies the other, such an alliance cannot last for a long time. As soon as the objectified person realizes he/she has been used to satisfy the fantasy of the other person, he/she will abruptly put an end to that objectification. Take for instance, if a married woman only likes her husband because of the expensive gifts he is buying for her, their relationship will soon hit the rock once the man finds out that he is only being valued as "Mr. Spender". Everyone wants to be unconditionally loved or appreciated in a relationship. Similarly, you cannot keep a woman for long if she realizes that she is only being valued for sexual pleasure.

- **Narcissistic partner:** As you are fully aware, a narcissistic person is completely self-centered, arrogant, and inconsiderate. A relationship works if the people involved in it value each other and mutually and show respect to one another. A narcissistic lover is only concerned about what he/she can get from the relationship.

He/she doesn't care if the other person is maltreated, under-appreciated, and manipulated. This accounts for why narcissistic individuals are not good at maintaining relationships.

- **Undue competitor:** When you are in a relationship whereby the other parties involved are unduly engaging in cutthroat competition with you, there are going to be some serious issues. A competitor wants to be better than you at all cost; so, instead of amicably dealing with things within the relationship, the other person will be forcing his/her ideas or opinions on you. That could set a dangerous pattern that may jeopardize the relationship, because no one admires being manipulated or ordered around.

- **A perfectionist:** No one is perfect; we all have our flaws as human beings. If you are in a relationship with a perfectionist, there is a tendency that such a relationship will soon collapse. Why? You cannot always have an unreasonable expectation of your partner—you must understand that people make mistakes. And that they should never be held hostage because of those mistakes. A lot of relationships could have been saved if the parties involved had exercised some patience with their partners.

You can see why there are so many relationship problems in the world. We are entering into relationships with people with different personalities and psychological makeups. This is why universal rela-tionship advice never works on all situations because people are psychologically different. You will save yourself some trouble if you can be patient enough to study your partner before heading into a relationship with him/her.

AMONGST YOUR FAMILY AND FRIENDS

There are also some forms of toxic and manipulative relationships among your family and friends.

Addressing his disciples in Matthew 10:36, Jesus Christ dropped a bombshell: *"a man's enemies will be the members of his own household."* This assertion has remained forever relevant even in our present age.

Do you know why? Your families and friends know a lot about you; they know your strengths and weaknesses. This gives them an edge over external manipulators if they choose to attack you with dark psychology. And if they do, you will feel the most pain from their attacks.

What could make your family and friends subject someone to dark psychology? You may want to know. There are a few reasons why your brother/sister or a close friend/acquaintance may want to harm or hurt you:

- **Envy:** If you happen to be more successful than some of your relatives or friends, they may be tempted to use dark psychology on you. Some of their attempts may be to lure you into giving them money or some pricey possessions they won't have had access to if they didn't use hypnotism or manipulative tactics on you. Sometimes, they may not want to see you die or be incapacitated, but their initial expectations could be that you become as hopeless as they are.

- **Competition:** There is usually a rivalry among siblings; your brother or sister will aspire to be better than you. In case they cannot achieve that naturally or by working hard, they may be tempted to give dark psychology a try.

- **Family discords:** There are many reasons why members of a family can become sworn enemies. Take for instance, when they are dividing their family properties after the demise of their parents, who did not leave a Will, they may do so disproportionately and cause one or more person to feel cheated in the process. The affected person (s) may resort to seeking justice through the use of dark psychology on any of his/her siblings.

The case is slightly different when it comes to friends and acquaintances. Your friends can only have as much information about you as you let them. And never forget that today's friend could be tomorrow's enemy. Warren G Harding once said, *"treat your friend as if he will one day be your enemy, and your enemy as if he will one day be your friend."*

In essence, the impacts a friend or an acquaintance can have on you depend how much you expose yourself to their influence. If you are a moderate person who doesn't make himself/herself vulnerable to friend-initiated dark psychology, you may be able to protect yourself from their evil intentions if they happen to think of hurting you.

Human beings are so unpredictable; so, do all you can to put yourself and your loved ones in a safe situation where unexpected dark psychological attacks will have no serious effects on you and your loved ones.

This doesn't mean that you should always suspect one or more of your friends as a potential manipulator; if you use your discretion very well, over time you can detect who is to be trusted and who to be sent packing from your life.

IN YOUR WORK

You can choose your friends and acquaintances, but you cannot, on most occasions, choose your co-workers. And there is nothing as difficult as working with manipulators. At first, they may disguise as a caring manager training you how to do some of the tasks assigned to you at the workplace. Over time, you will see that they are becoming more demanding and manipulative in nature.

Unfortunately, a large number of female employees have been harassed by their superiors who wanted more than just working with them. And if a female employee refuses sexual advances from a male superior, he may make life difficult for her.

You surely have some well-defined options when it comes to dealing with a manipulator at work. Here are some time-tested approaches you can adopt to proactively deal with a manipulator at your workplace:

- **Compose yourself:** Understand the fact that no company

or office welcomes heartless manipulators; you are, to some degree, protected by your company's rules, irrespective of the position of the manipulator. So, compose yourself. Ask sensible questions to clarify whatever the manipulator might be querying you for. Of course, a male manager that wants to sleep with his subordinate, who is a female worker, will never say it directly. Instead, he will be accusing her from time to time for not doing her job very well. So, ask relevant questions to clarify the issue under discussion. If necessary, involve another high-ranking manager in the discussion.

- **Stay away from the manipulator:** If you can, always stay away from the manipulator. You can request to have your seat rearranged so that you are not always sitting next to him/her. When in meetings, do not attempt to interrupt the manipulator so that you don't give them the chance to lambast or attack you in meetings.

- **Don't say "Yes" to everything:** Honestly, you don't have to say "yes" to every task given to you by the manipulator who keeps looking for an opportunity to attack you. You can claim that you are busy on a task so that they look around for another person to take it up. Remember that your colleagues are not your friends nor family members; interact with them with caution. If a sex-obsessed senior executive is asking you out to drink with him, you have the right to say "No!".

- **Know Your Rights:** Don't forget that you have rights at your workplace. So, if you are sure someone is pressing you too hard to compromise your integrity, you can complain to the establishment using their normal procedures for registering grievances. It is dangerous to keep enduring harassment and manipulation at work, thinking that the perpetrator will change. That's an erroneous thinking, because most manipulators are excited seeing their victims in pain.

CAN THEY STILL CHANGE?

It is common among victims of manipulation to assume that their manipulators can still change. Will they? Well, there are some instances why they may. We are talking about salvaging relationships that shouldn't have, in the first place, turned sour. A husband and a wife can choose to reconcile after discovering that they were both at fault. An employee can forgive an erring employer and reconcile with him/her. Some relations and friends may have learned that their actions were wrong and have duly apologized for their misdemeanors.

However, be careful! Not everyone who apologizes really means it; some old friends or associates may reconcile with you because they realise they cannot enjoy similar benefits they have been having without you. So, use your discretion in each circumstance.

Can all manipulators still change? The answer is an emphatic "NO!" Some evil-minded people who approach you for the singular purpose of hurting you, defrauding you of your prized possessions, or even taking your precious life will never see any reasons to leave you alone. Those are the categories of manipulative people that you should never give a second chance, because they will hurt you more.

DEFENDING YOURSELF AGAINST MANIPULATORS

The best way to defend yourself against evil manipulators is to not give them unfettered access to you. Keep them far away from you. Don't be that kind-hearted person who is always willing to give people a second chance without finding out, beforehand, if they are going to add value to your life or business.

Always remember that you have nothing to gain from manipulating and toxic relationships. So, take the steps to protect yourself from toxic relationships:

- Get out of any relationships that do not serve your purpose.
- Do not let your colleagues or acquaintances know your weaknesses; they could use them to manipulate you.
- Identify the purposes of a relationship before starting it; if your interest is not clearly expressed in the agreement, get out of the relationship.
- Never allow a manipulator to get a chance into entering your life without knowing if he/she has something good to add to your life.
- Use your discretions and natural instincts to spot out manipulators far before they attack you. Chances are that you will always have a natural way to identify a mischievous troublemaker before he/she makes his/her tent in your life.
- Stop making yourself vulnerable to dark psychologists' attacks. The easiest way people expose themselves to danger is to present themselves as emotional and weak.

14

AGAINST ONLINE ATTACKS

Dark psychologists have gone a new platform for launching their debilitating attacks—the internet. In recent years, lives of some innocent people have been turned upside down due to the nefarious activities of online manipulators. This malicious practice is called cyberbullying, whereby a handful of evil-intentioned people hide behind the anonymity of the internet to bully or attempt to manipulate the behaviors of others.

The 2020 statistics on cyberbullying is pathetic: About 36.5 percent of people reported being bullied online in their lifetime, while 17. 4 percent confessed that it has occurred to them in the last 30 days. And 87 percent of young people complained to have been bullied mainly on online platforms.

The impacts of these evil online practices are as well significant: About 64 percent of those who are bullied say that they do not feel safe at schools. And they exhibit some social and mental health issues if the bullying persists longer than expected. To manage their situations, many cyberbullied people often take to excessive drinking or abuse substances. In serious circumstances, they could commit suicide or harm others in their vicinities.

FACTS AND LIES

Internet is still pretty much an open platform that is poorly regulated. This entails that much of the information online is not moderated. This gives the opportunity for those with evil intentions to easily spread lies about others. Most of them get away with the falsehoods they are broadcasting, except in rare cases when the attention of the moderator of the platform is drawn to the content, which they will later make an effort to delete.

The idea of fake news further exacerbates the reliability of the online platforms. Sometimes even governmental agencies spread rumors to deceive unsuspicious citizens. Before he was voted out of office, Donald Trump and his administrative officers held sway over ordinary Americans that it was even difficult for them to differentiate truths from lies. In the same way, other organizations have released untrue information online that are publicly quoted by people all over the world who do not have the resources to confirm if the information was true or not.

You may be confused about what you should believe on the internet then. Well, some decorum is finding its way to the internet and social media companies are increasingly working round the clock to strike out fake news, destructive information, and unconfirmed rumors from their platforms.

Before you believe anything online, use these yardsticks to help you separate truths from half-truths or lies:

- **Authority sources:** Make sure the information you are spreading is coming from the authority sources. Take for instance, you could see a blue tick (v) beside the name of the person or organization releasing that information. This means that those sources have been confirmed to be real/true by the social media companies.
- **Believable experiences/stories:** You can also help yourself only to the truth online by accepting believable stories. These are factual stories that are almost always true. Take for instance, if someone says the Sun rises in the East and sets in the West, you probably don't need to fact-check that because it is the truth.
- **Confirmed information:** Sometimes you may not know the sources of some information. But if they have been confirmed by other authority sources, that piece of information could be true. For example, you may not know who said something many years ago, but if a reliable person quoted the same statement that was made many years ago, the truthfulness of the statement can be attributed to the reliable personality that authenticates it.
- **Well-known facts:** You may not need to fact-check well-known facts. We all understand that some religious data or

information are incontestable. In that scenario, you can save yourself some time to clarify them.

That being said, internet is still a very dangerous place that one must carefully navigate, most especially for little children.

BE AWARE OF DARK PATTERNS

When you search online for any service, you must be careful who is responding to your call for help. The anonymity of the internet has made it possible for dark psychologists to hide behind a computer screen and secretly find their ways into people lives.

According to FBI, the internet crime rate has increased proportionately in the past years. In 2019 alone, there were 467, 361 internet crime complaints made, which translated into 1,300 complaints per day. In total, there was an estimated $3.5 billion losses to businesses and individuals.

The nature of the crime committed online is getting darker each day, from a pedophile lurking in the dark looking for kids to prey on to dark psychologists making continuous attempts to manipulate people with the click of a mouse. From dating sites, many unconscious lovers have thrown themselves into the arms of manipulators who make their lives truly unbearable. Many manipulative and toxic relationships are being formed every day, and people do not necessarily seem to have learned any lessons.

So, what should you in the face of mounting takeover of the internet by the dark psychologists? Well, there is no one-size-fits-all answer in this regard. But, as you will soon discover, there are steps you can take to protect yourself and your loved ones online.

Keeping yourself safe is a daily battle you must wage. The internet is a large ocean full of malicious sharks. And what they are looking for is you, your property, your heart, or somehow your life. It is your responsibility to make sure they don't get whatever they think they are looking for.

For you to know how dark the internet is becoming, young people are facing an unprecedented level of threats online. In an interview conducted to find out about how some teens were bullied online, the following observations were made: And the most common kinds of cyberbullying teens experience include:

- Offensive name-calling (42%)
- Spreading of false rumors (32%)
- Receiving explicit images, they didn't ask for (25%)
- Constant asking of who they are, what they're doing, and who they're with by someone other than a parent (21%)
- Physical threats (16%)
- Having explicit images shared without their consent (7%)

MANIPULATIVE INFORMATION

Most of the fake news or information online are directed at certain groups of people, and their covert purpose is to manipulate them. Take for instance, there are certain categories of people called the Leftist and Rightist. These groups constantly produce online content that will solidify their socio-political beliefs, convictions, and ideologies. It doesn't matter if the messages they are sending out are true or false; what is important to them is to continue to control the thoughts of their followings, telling them exactly whatever they are waiting to hear and totally brainwash them.

Recently, people are subscribing to websites that offer daily horoscopes. The most shocking aspect of this is that they absolutely believe everything they read about their stars, whether they are Aries, Scorpio, or Capricorn. Through this holistic adhere to horoscope and reading of tarot cards, some people have carelessly made themselves vulnerable to dark psychologists' attacks.

More so, dark patterns are noticeable in some online marketing and advertising. People are being manipulated to reluctantly spend their hard-earned money on things they don't need in the first place. A blogger lists some of the tactics employed by dark marketers to manipulate buyers, and they include:

1. **Trick questions:** Buyers are asked some tricky questions they may not have answers for. In the course of that, they may be lured into paying for goods they don't really want.
2. **Sneak into basket:** This is a deceptive and manipulative practice whereby online shoppers are tricked into buying something because the algorithm has suggested them to be useful alongside a good product they are purchasing.
3. **Roach motel:** This is a kind of cockroach bait used to catch the insect. In this case, a roach motel could mean disguising a

178 | DARK PSYCHOLOGY AND MANIPULATION PROTECTION 2 I...

product as very attractive only to compel shoppers to click on buying it.

4. **Privacy Zuckering:** This is a typical dark pattern that has received much attention lately. E-commerce or online stores sometimes add a hidden line to their "terms and conditions" which allows them to secretly sell customers' or shoppers' private information to a third-party.

5. **Price comparison prevention:** Sometimes shoppers are deceived into believing that they are getting the best price on a product. Why? Because shopping marketplaces or the search engines have hidden comparison of prices from them. So, they are not aware that there are other online stores offering the same products at a cheaper price.

6. **Misdirection:** More often than not, shoppers are misdirected while navigating an online store. They could receive suggestions about useless products that they don't need.

7. **Hidden costs:** What makes online manipulation worse, as far as online shopping is concerned, are the hidden costs storeowners sometime include in the price lists. If you are not careful, you may end up paying more for a product that it actually worth.

8. **Bait and switch:** This is an advertising dark pattern that has been in practice for ages. In this case, a store advertises a product at a bargain price. And when buyers purchased them, they are sent counterfeit products with poor value. Sometimes, shoppers may not be able to differentiate the

original from their counterfeit products because they look exactly alike.

9. **Confirmshaming:** Some online stores shame shoppers from confirming their final list of purchased products in their shopping cart. They do this to intentionally defraud them, adding hidden costs to the final price paid for the shopping.

10. **Disguised ads:** These ads are disguised as content from another source, meanwhile they are placed on a store by the storeowner. So, when a potential shopper sees it, he/she may be excited to shop elsewhere, without knowing that the same store owns the ads.

11. **Forced continuity:** Nowadays, storeowners can use algorithms that can urge shoppers to continue shopping. This dark pattern is referred to as forced continuity, because if the shopper wants to exit shopping, he/she will be directed to another listing page on the store.

12. **Friend spam:** Have you ever been a store and you suddenly see a pop-up that says, "Your friend has bought this!"? This dark practice is called friend spam—because stores will spam you based on the products your friends have purchased previously.

It is apparent from the examples provided in this section that internet remains a dangerous medium that is full of countless manipulative tactics. From dating, horoscopes, to online shopping. In this dispensation, you can also learn about Neuro-linguistic programming (NLP) online or join an association of witches/wizards or Satanism right on the internet. The dangers posed by all these online interactions are enormous.

MAKE CHECKING FACTS A HABIT

The truth is that you don't want to become a victim of all these online manipulations. The first place to start in protecting yourself is not to believe everything you see on the internet. Fact-check every piece of information to make sure it is originating from a very reliable source. Do not follow the crowd to embrace a new technology without confirming that it has something good to offer you.

Today, there are millions of online thought leaders and influencers. You don't have to follow any of them if they don't preach the causes you are passionate about. Some of the online motivators are, in fact, manipulators in disguise because they will force you to practice their mantras from time to time. Some of them will even take the conversation with you out of the internet and start calling you to get a better grip on your life.

You can avoid plunging yourself into misfortune by questioning the veracity of the things you see online. Lately, prostitutes don't advertise their services openly; they will put a deceptive advertisement on the internet, like "Get in touch with us for your body health services!" Body health services? Yes, that is how crafty and dodgy manipulators are. And when you fall into their hands, they will control you like a baby!

You are one of the luckiest beings on earth for reading this. According to the great physicist, Galileo Galilei, "*all truths are easy to under-*

stand once they are discovered, the point is to discover them."
You should make it your duty to always seek the truth because, as the
Bible says, only the truth can set you free.

Use the following four essential steps to confirm the veracity of
anything you see on the internet:

- **Step 1: Identify spurious or fake content:** Always be
  alert. When you see a piece of information that seems to be
  too good to be true, let your fact-checking instinct come
  alive.
- **Step 2: Verify the source of the information:** You
  may need to look at the link that carries the message,
  investigate the author of the information, the date it was
  published, contact information of the author, and see
  whether the author is an authority on the subject-matter.
  This technique can help you screen out fluffy content.
- **Step 3: Check out if the content is relevant:** You may
  want to confirm if the content is accurate, recent, and
  applicable to the purpose you want to use it for. Is it some
  practical report, a satire, or an imitation?
- **Step 4: Weigh the veracity of the evidence:** Is the
  evidence portrayed in the information correct? Are there
  similar citations that could prove that the information
  released on the internet is true and not fake?

If you patiently followed the four steps highlighted above, you will be
able to reduce the number of falsehoods you consume on the internet.

This will help you to concentrate on nothing but the truths and protect yourself from dark psychologists' attacks.

PROTECTING YOURSELF ONLINE

To some extent, you can protect yourself online. Apart from bookmarking most of the useful online content that you would like to access from time to time, there are further actions to safeguard yourself while on the internet.

Outlined below are ten practical approaches you could use to protect yourself online:

- Never open emails or messages from strangers. Many people who got themselves into trouble with manipulators started by communicating with them online, without first knowing or meeting them.
- You should make sure that your devices have up-to-date security protections. That will help you keep malware, spyware, and hackers at bay.
- Make sure you are using strong passwords that cannot be easily compromised.
- You should use two-factor authentication on all of your online sign-ins. This will prevent any impostors getting into your systems and stealing your vital data.
- Refrain from clicking on all links that appear strange; they could be a virus or a hacker looking for a way to get into your system.
- It is not advisable that you should use public WIFI that is

mostly unprotected. Malware or spyware can get into your system through that.

- Make it a habit to back up your data regularly. When your system is down and requires a reboot, you may have back-up data to use.
- Be careful not to expose your financial information online. Internet criminals can get valuable information from your computing system and use it against you.
- You should educate every member of your family how to play safe on the internet.
- Never share your personal information with anyone. Some careless people who freely provide their private information to strangers have ended up becoming victims of online manipulations.

Above all, use your discretion and stay safe. Most of the precautions described in this book are doable only if you try them.

15

IMPROVING YOUR EMOTIONAL INTELLIGENCE

The most important thing you should concentrate on improving is **Yourself!** Why? No amount of evil intentions the dark psychologists plan towards you will work if you have high emotional intelligence.

The Oxford Learners' Dictionary defines "Emotional Intelligence" as *"the ability to understand your emotions and those of other people and to behave appropriately in different situations."* With good emotional intelligence, you will know the right thing to do at the right time to save your life. Unfortunately, not everyone has great emotional intelligence. Some people still need to work on themselves to improve their emotional intelligence.

WHY IMPROVE?

It is imperative that you improve your emotional intelligence so that you will be able to withstand whatever tricks the dark psychologists are playing on you. Why Improve?" No one can help you if you don't help yourself first. And the main way to help yourself is to do everything in your power to better protect yourself against dark psychology. And you can accomplish this by tuning up your emotional capability.

People need high emotional intelligence because:

- They need to handle all things that come their way in life, and they should be able to perform sensibly when under stress.
- They need to ward off potential manipulators who may be looking around for emotionally weak individuals to manipulate their thoughts and actions.
- They can apply their instincts to issues and resolve problems quickly without losing much or nothing at all in the process.
- High emotional intelligent people are fully in charge of their senses when in any circumstances. In other words, their actions are not influenced by external forces.
- They can identify problems in the distance and do whatever it takes to avoid it.

TAKE AN EMOTIONAL INTELLIGENCE (EI) TEST

How do you know your emotional intelligence (EI) level? You should take an emotional intelligence test or a combination of emotional intelligence tests. The outcome(s) of these tests will show how emotionally resilient you are to handle all difficult issues life will bring your way.

An individual can measure his/her emotional intelligence through three unique techniques:

- **By using a self-report or self-assessment**
- **By using other reports conducted by a third-party**
- **By utilizing ability measurement tools**

A number of tools have been developed by different organizations to accomplish the task of measuring a person's emotional intelligence. They include questionnaires, quizzes, and scales. There are four main classes of intelligence that are measured by different tests; they include:

- **Abilities-based tests**
- **Trait (or character)-based tests**
- **Competency-based tests**
- **Behavior-based tests**

Emotional intelligence (EI) scales: There are different scales developed for the purpose of measuring people's emotional intelligence. The most commonly applied EI scale is a 33-item scale purportedly designed from studies carried out by Schuette and colleagues in 1998, which was an adaptation from the 64-item scale previously published in 1990 by Salovey and Mayer.

Here is the 33-item emotional intelligence scale upon which people's emotional resiliency is measured:

1. I know when to speak about my personal problems to others.
2. When I am faced with obstacles, I remember times I faced similar obstacles and overcame them.
3. I expect that I will do well on most things I try.
4. Other people find it easy to confide in me.
5. I find it hard to understand the non-verbal messages of other people.
6. Some of the major events of my life have led me to re-evaluate what is important and not important.
7. When my mood changes, I see new possibilities.
8. Emotions are one of the things that make my life worth living.
9. I am aware of my emotions as I experience them.
10. I expect good things to happen.
11. I like to share my emotions with others.
12. When I experience a positive emotion, I know how to make it last.
13. I arrange events others enjoy.
14. I seek out activities that make me happy.
15. I am aware of the non-verbal messages I send to others.

16. I present myself in a way that makes a good impression on others.

17. When I am in a positive mood, solving problems is easy for me.

18. By looking at their facial expressions, I recognize the emotions people are experiencing.

19. I know why my emotions change.

20. When I am in a positive mood, I am able to come up with new ideas.

21. I have control over my emotions.

22. I easily recognize my emotions as I experience them.

23. I motivate myself by imagining a good outcome to tasks I take on.

24. I compliment others when they have done something well.

25. I am aware of the non-verbal messages other people send.

26. When another person tells me about an important event in his or her life, I almost feel as though I have experienced this event myself.

27. When I feel a change in emotions, I tend to come up with new ideas.

28. When I am faced with a challenge, I give up because I believe I will fail.

29. I know what other people are feeling just by looking at them.

30. I help other people feel better when they are down.

31. I use good moods to help myself keep trying in the face of obstacles.

32. I can tell how people are feeling by listening to the tone of their voice.

33. It is difficult for me to understand why people feel the way they do.

Emotional Intelligence (EI) Questionnaires: These are questionnaires specifically designed to measure people's EI. One of such a questionnaire, designed by Mind Tools (2019) is provided below for your use:

Note: Responders are encouraged to offer true answers to the statements below as they are currently, and not as they hope they could be:

1. I can recognize my emotions as I experience them.
2. I lose my temper when I feel frustrated.
3. People have told me that I'm a good listener.
4. I know how to calm myself down when I feel anxious or upset.
5. I enjoy organizing groups.
6. I find it hard to focus on something over the long term.
7. I find it difficult to move on when I feel frustrated or unhappy.
8. I know my strengths and weaknesses.
9. I avoid conflict and negotiations.
10. I feel that I don't enjoy my work.
11. I ask people for feedback on what I do well, and how I can improve.
12. I set long-term goals and review my progress regularly.
13. I find it difficult to read other people's emotions.
14. I struggle to build rapport with others.
15. I use active listening skills when people speak to me.

For each of these statements, the responders would rate themselves from not at all, rarely, sometimes, often and very often (Mind Tools, 2019).

Emotional Intelligence (EI) Quiz: Quizzes are also popularly used to measure people's intelligence. The sample quiz below is developed by Institute for Health and Human Potential.

Statement: I do not become defensive when criticized.

Possible answers: Strongly agree, Agree, Neither agree nor disagree, Disagree, and Strongly disagree.

Note: Your choice of answer can say a lot about you and your temperament. And these are the interpretations for each selected answer:

Strong Agree: I utilize criticism and other feedback for growth.

Agree: I am positive.

Neither agree nor disagree: I maintain a sense of humor.

Disagree: I try to see things from another's perspective.

Strongly disagree: I recognize how my behavior affects others.

Emotional Intelligence Quadrants: This comprises of four distinct quadrants that measure each aspect of human intelligence, namely self-awareness, social awareness, relationship management, and self-management.

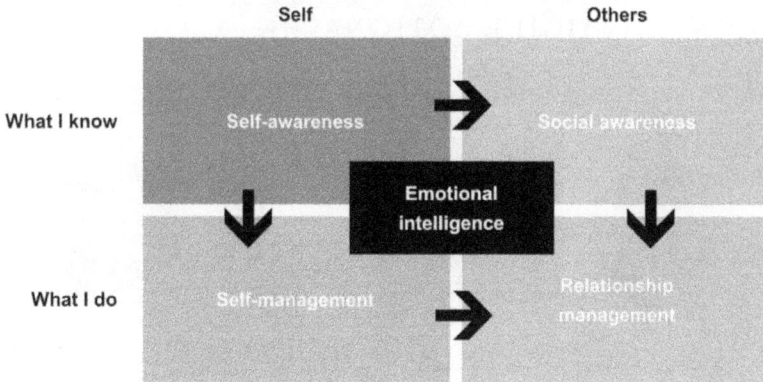

Emotional Intelligence Score: Each emotional intelligence test has its own scoring system. You can either have a high or a low score. When your score is low; all you need to do is to check the areas where your scores are low and do something about strengthening or improving upon those areas. When you work on improving yourself for some time, you can come back to take the test (s) after several weeks of self-development to see how you will do again in the tests.

The primary purpose of taking an Emotional Intelligence test is to let you know which aspects of your life is weak and may be taken advantage of by dark psychologists.

5 SIGNS OF HIGH EMOTIONAL INTELLIGENCE

When your emotional intelligence is pretty high, you will be able to do the following very well:

- **Good decision-making:** Your decisions about every area of your life will be spot on and powerful.
- **Better stress management:** You will demonstrate high resiliency that is useful in proactively managing stress.
- **Improved interpersonal skills:** Your interpersonal skills will improve dramatically.
- **Self-perception:** You will always see yourself in a better light and hold yourself at high esteem.
- **Self-expression:** You will be able to express yourself confidently and purposefully.

HOW TO IMPROVE?

Having seen how important high emotional intelligence is, it is imperative that you should do everything in your power to improve your emotional intelligence. You can take some of the steps described below to achieve that:

professional success. Below are 10 ways to increase your EQ:

1. Communicate boldly.

Let your communication with people be assertive and sensible. If you are too passive, people around you may misunderstand your good intentions.

2. Respond, don't react to stressor.

When you find yourself in a situation where your emotional resolve is being tested with conflicts and stress, do not react but respond accordingly. Let people see you as reasonable and calm in any situations.

3. Better listening skills.

It is usually said that intelligent people listen when discuss with people so that they can obtain clear messages and respond sensibly. If you are talkative and never listen to what the others are saying, your answers might be inappropriate for issues under discussion and people might consider you to be of low emotional intelligence.

4. Always be motivated.

Self-motivation is the key; don't wait until people come around to motivate you. You are your own savior when it comes to adopting coping strategies to deal with life's uncertainties.

5. Always maintain a positive attitude.

Let it be part and parcel of your attitude to constantly maintain a positive attitude about things. Because being overtly negative can affect your mental health and destabilize everything about you.

6. Practice regular self-awareness.

If you know who you are, no one can underestimate your worth. Most of the people who become victims of manipulations are those who are self-effaced and don't particularly know their self-worth.

7. Calmly accept criticism.

The easiest way to test anyone's emotional intelligence is to see how they react when criticized. If you are a boisterous arguer who won't let people get a word in edgeways, you may be excluded from many intelligent discussions because people can't handle your vituperation when angered.

8. Be empathetic.

One of the best qualities of emotionally intelligent people is that they show empathy to people around them. They share in their weaknesses and feel like they are in the same unfortunate position as the people they are sympathizing with.

9. Use your leadership skills.

It is important that you use your leadership skills wherever you find yourself. You won't always be a subordinate; so, when a duty of honor comes up, act as honorable as possible. Take for instance, if you are a senior executive in a company, it is your responsibility to calmly attend to the needs of those working under you, including showing them a great example of leadership.

10. Be approachable and sociable.

If you are cantankerous and always pick quarrels with people, you may not be perceived as someone with high emotional intelligence.

IT TAKES TIME AND PRACTICE

Can you learn how to improve your emotional intelligence? Definitely. The good news is that people are not born with high emotional intelligence; they most learn them, as you would study any subject at school. However, it takes time and practice to get good at it. It requires consistent practice for it to be truly developed.

You can use the following techniques to develop your emotional intelligence:

- **Understanding your emotions.** Analyse each of your emotions and understand how to use them well. So many things in your life will go wrong if you misapply your emotions. Keep quiet where you are supposed to hold your peace. Never be overanxious about things that do not matter and protect yourself from manipulators who are always looking for those who are too emotional.

- **Matching your emotions to the right scenarios:** After analyzing your emotions, you will fully understand which emotion to use in a certain circumstance. In this case, match your emotions with the applicable tasks and scenarios. This will help you to do the right thing at the right time.

- **Map your emotions:** Sometimes you may need to map your emotions and put them under control when necessary. This entails that you interact with individuals based on their relevance at a particular point in time. You cannot transfer emotion to those who do not merit it. For example, you cannot use the emotion for a business partner with your child. Such inappropriate use of emotion will point you out as immature. In reality, people have a measure of expectation from everyone; it is in your power to decide who gets what. It is practically unreasonable to be angry with a person who has not offended you in anyway. If that happens, people will have every reason to doubt your emotional intelligence.

CONCLUSION

After reading this book with detailed information about how to deal with the threats all of us face every day, you should be really happy for the deep knowledge you have garnered from it. It is almost impossible to find a book out there that exhaustively treats the subject-matter of dark psychology as much as this book does.

No one should ever be subjected to the dehumanizing experiences of manipulation, hypnotism, and destructive Neuro-Linguistic Programming. Instead of keeping quiet and letting people be treated in a way that undermine their human rights and humanity, I took upon myself to write this book. Take this as a warning for you and your loved ones, because if you could judiciously follow the comprehensively researched content in this book, you will be better off after digesting it.

When someone is ill, they can go to see the doctor for a cure. Unfortunately, most of the people who have been or are currently being manipulated don't realize they are victims. They think it is a natural experience that they must go through. Good thing, this book will serve as an eye-opener for many victims who still don't know that their lives could have been more glorified than they are now if they had learned about manipulators years before.

This is not a book that should be read one time and dumped on a shelf; you should constantly consult it so that you could continuously gain insights into the machinations of dark psychologists and remain ahead of them in the curve of personal development. You have got to do what it takes to remain in a safe position, while helping friends and relatives to discover the same safe haven offered in this book.

The topics covered in this book are evergreen, always applicable to our day-to-day survival in this wild world. Keep digesting all the important information about how you can master your emotions, improve your emotional intelligence, identify manipulators, hypnotists, and NLP practitioners. Prevention is the best method for safety. As long as you. are armed with the cogent information highlighted in this book, you will be able to ward off dark psychologists by doing things that will frustrate their moves towards you and your loved ones.

You have a lot to lose by allowing a dark psychologist to enter into you. It may already be late to redress the situation. An average dark psychologist has an evil intention they want to actualize on their victims. Many people have lost valuable properties, wealth and, in some serious circumstance, their precious lives. You only live once; it is your perpetual responsibility to keep yourself and your loved ones safe.

You can as well see this book as pages of life coaching about the dangers of dark psychologists and how to avoid them. This will help you to actively visualize the information in the pages. They must be engrained in your mind from time to time so that they can be useful for you.

I think you should congratulate yourself; The first step in defeating evil is to know, in detail, how they operate. Then you will use your knowledge about them to disarm and frustrate them.

Do not hesitate to share the invaluable knowledge in this book with your friends, loved ones, and acquaintances. Doing so, you might be able to save someone's life. Dark psychology is pretty much in use on a large scale in our world. It is through this level of education about their influence that we could all work together to put an end of their menace.

Apart from that, people will continue to fall victims to dark psychologists, who run into millions all over the world.

RESOURCES

Beheshti, N. (2020, May 15). Toxic influence: An average of 80% Americans have experienced emotional abuse. (https://www.forbes.com/sites/nazbeheshti/2020/05/15/an-average-of-80-of-americans-have-experienced-emotional-abuse/?sh=565b44067b49

Birkett, A. (2020, September 5). Online manipulation: All the ways you're currently being deceived. Online Manipulation: All The Ways You're Currently Being Deceived (cxl.com)

Britannica (2021). Hypnosis. https://www.britannica.com/science/hypnosis

Broadband Search (2021). 51 critical cyberbullying statistics in 2020. 51 Critical Cyberbullying Statistics in 2020 - BroadbandSearch

Clark, J. (2021). What are emotions, and why do we have them? https://science.howstuffworks.com/life/what-are-emotions.htm

Cohut, M. (2017, September 1). Hypnosis: What is it, and how does it work? https://www.medicalnewstoday.com/articles/319251

Cook, S. (2021, February 7). Cyberbullying facts and statistics for 2018-2021. Cyberbullying Statistics and Facts for 2021 | Comparitech

Cowen, A. (2018, May 9). How many different kinds of emotions are there? http://kids.frontiersin.org/article/10.3389/frym.2018.00015

Daskal, L. (2016, March 31). How to make yourself mentally strong this year: These 15 habits will you keep you at your sharpest, whatever comes your way. https://www.inc.com/lolly-daskal/how-to-make-yourself-mentally-strong-this-year.html

Federal Bureau of Investigation (2020, February 11). 2019 internet crime report released. 2019 Internet Crime Report Released — FBI

Global Investigation (2021). Infidelity statistics in the UK (Infographic).Infidelity Statistics in the UK [Infographic] – Global Investigations

GoodTherapy (2019, March 26). Manipulation. https://www.goodtherapy.org/blog/psychpedia/manipulation

GoodTherapy (2018, December 2). Neuro-Linguistic Programming (NLP). https://www.goodtherapy.org/learn-about-therapy/types/neuro-linguistic-programming

Goulston, M. (2013, December 19). Never be manipulated again. https://www.psychologytoday.com/us/blog/just-listen/201312/never-be-manipulated-again

Jones, J. (2021). Dark psychology & manipulation: Are you unknowingly using them? https://drjasonjones.com/dark_psychology/

Kaufman, S.B. (2019, March 19). The light triad vs. dark triad of personality: New research contrasts two different profiles of human nature. https://blogs.scientificamerican.com/beautiful-minds/the-light-triad-vs-dark-triad-of-personality/

Lidow, D. (2019, August 11). We must curtail online manipulation before it's too late: Here are four things we can do. https://www.forbes.com/sites/dereklidow/2019/08/11/we-must-curtail-online-manipulation-before-its-too-late-here-are-four-things-we-can-do/?sh=44b80aa7e000

Living Without Abuse (2021). Statistics. Domestic Abuse Statistics | lwa.org.uk : LWA

Louv, J. (2021). 10 ways to protect yourself from NLP mind control. https://ultraculture.org/blog/2014/01/16/nlp-10-ways-protect-mind-control/

Mental health.gov (2020, May 28). What is mental health? https://www.mentalhealth.gov/basics/what-is-mental-health

Mind Tools (2021). Understanding the dark triad: Managing "dark" personality traits. https://www.mindtools.com/pages/article/understanding-dark-triad.htm

Morgan, N. (2017, April 20). Why learn about body language? Here's one reason. https://publicwords.com/2017/04/20/learn-body-language-heres-one-reason/

Naim, R. (2016, April 25). 10 types of people you don't really need in your life. https://thoughtcatalog.com/rania-naim/2016/04/10-types-of-people-you-really-dont-need-in-your-life/

Ni, P. (2014, June 1). How to spot and stop manipulators. https://www.psychologytoday.com/us/blog/communication-success/201406/how-spot-and-stop-manipulators

NLP-TECHNIQUES. ORG (2021). What is NLP? NLP Techniques. NLP training. NLP coaching. https://www.nlp-techniques.org/

Office Dynamics International (2013, September 8). Persuasion skill—the good, the bad, and the ugly. https://officedynamics.com/persuasion-skills-the-good-the-bad-and-the-ugly/

Overby, S. (2019, June 6). Can emotional intelligence be learned? 4 techniques to practice. https://enterprisersproject.com/article/2019/6/can-emotional-intelligence-be-learned-4-techniques

Parvez, H. (2015, April 16). What is the importance of learning body language? https://www.psychmechanics.com/importance-of-learning-body-language/

Psychologia (2021). Infographic: Psychological manipulation. https://psychologia.co/emotional-manipulation/

Psychology Today (2021). Emotional Intelligence Test. https://www.psychologytoday.com/us/tests/personality/emotional-intelligence-test

Quora (2021). What's dark psychology? https://www.quora.com/Whats-dark-psychology

Quora (2021). When is persuasion a form od bad manipulation? https://www.quora.com/When-is-persuasion-a-form-of-bad-manipulation

University of Minnesota (2021). How do thoughts and emotions affect health? https://www.takingcharge.csh.umn.edu/how-do-thoughts-and-emotions-affect-health

Villines, Z. (2019, September 17). Red flags: Are you being emotionally manipulated? https://www.goodtherapy.org/blog/red-flags-are-you-being-emotionally-manipulated-0917197

Wildenberg, L. (2017, May 5). 10 types of people you don't need in your life. https://www.crosswalk.com/slideshows/10-types-of-people-you-don-t-need-in-your-life.html

www.ingramcontent.com/pod-product-compliance
Lightning Source LLC
Chambersburg PA
CBHW030243030426
42336CB00009B/235